James E. Smith

A Famous Battery and its Campaigns - 1861-'64

The career of Corporal James Tanner in war and in peace - Vol. 2

James E. Smith

A Famous Battery and its Campaigns - 1861-'64
The career of Corporal James Tanner in war and in peace - Vol. 2

ISBN/EAN: 9783337222680

Printed in Europe, USA, Canada, Australia, Japan

Cover: Foto ©Andreas Hilbeck / pixelio.de

More available books at **www.hansebooks.com**

JAMES E. SMITH.

A
FAMOUS BATTERY

AND

ITS CAMPAIGNS, 1861-'64

THE CAREER OF
CORPORAL JAMES TANNER
IN WAR AND IN PEACE

EARLY DAYS IN THE BLACK HILLS
WITH SOME ACCOUNT OF
CAPT. JACK CRAWFORD
The Poet Scout

BY

CAPTAIN JAMES E. SMITH
4th N. Y. Independent Battery

WASHINGTON
W. H. LOWDERMILK & CO.
1892

Copyright, 1892, by JAMES E. SMITH

PREFACE

In presenting these memoirs to the public my aim is simply a plain, unvarnished tale to tell of the gallant deeds of a Battery which, to use the words of the official report of the Adjutant-General of the State of New York (Vol. I, page 169, 1868), "served during the war with as bright a record as any in the whole Army," and, incidentally, to correct some erroneous statements and reports in the light of the fuller information now attainable regarding the tremendous events of the memorable epoch in our Nation's history to which they relate.

This sketch of its marches from the uplands of Bull Run to the swamps of the Chickahominy, from the malarious Peninsula to the breezy Pennsylvania hills, is measurably a contemporaneous history of the battles of the Army of the Potomac, for there were but few of them that this Battery did not participate in. I have endeavored to state facts, and trust that the verdict of my readers may be: "He nothing extenuated, nor aught set down in malice."

J. E. S.

A FAMOUS BATTERY

CONTENTS.

PART I.

THE THREE MONTHS' SERVICE IN VARIAN'S BATTERY.

CHAPTER I 1
Southward Ho!—An unrecorded engagement.

CHAPTER II 6
In Camp at Annapolis.—A tilt with General Butler.

CHAPTER III 12
On Picket in Virginia.—Cub Run.—Home Again.

CHAPTER IV 24
Some Personal Incidents.

PART II.

THE FOURTH NEW YORK BATTERY—ITS FORMATION, ITS SERVICES, AND ITS DISSOLUTION.

CHAPTER I 33
Organization.—On to Washington.

CHAPTER II 43
Winter Quarters in Lower Maryland.—Incidents.

CONTENTS.

CHAPTER III 51
    Yorktown.

CHAPTER IV 57
    Williamsburg.

CHAPTER V 66
    Official Reports.—Some misstatements corrected.

CHAPTER VI 82
    Fredericksburg.

CHAPTER VII 93
    After Fredericksburg.—A Summer March through Maryland.

CHAPTER VIII 101
    Gettysburg.

CHAPTER IX 113
    Official Reports.—Union.

CHAPTER X 123
    Official Reports.—Confederate.

CHAPTER XI 133
    Letters from participants in the battle referring to the part taken by the Battery.

CHAPTER XII 147
    Remarks and Criticisms.

CHAPTER XIII 156
    Poetic Tributes to the Battery.—I. *A Famous Battery and its Day of Glory,* by Capt. Jack Crawford, the Poet Scout.—II. *Devil's Den,* by Comrade Samuel Adams Wiggin.

CHAPTER XIV 164
    Back to Washington.—Disbanded.

APPENDIX	175
THE CAREER OF CORPORAL TANNER . .	179
EARLY DAYS IN THE BLACK HILLS	217
THE GRAND ARMY OF THE REPUBLIC . . .	235

PART I

THE THREE MONTHS SERVICE IN VARIAN'S BATTERY

CHAPTER I

Southward, Ho!—An Unrecorded Engagement

LONG before the first rays of the sun had glinted on the topmasts of the shipping in New York Harbor, in the early dawn of April 19, 1861, the old "Washington Gray Troop," or Company "I" of the 8th New York State Militia, reorganized the day before as Varian's Battery of Light Artillery, started for "the front"—magic words in the feverish days of the early sixties, that made the blood dance in the veins, and filled the souls of the average young man of that period with a wild longing for the stirring life of the camp and the battlefield.

We were on board the steamship *Montgomery* under sealed orders, and our destination was — well, somewhere in the tumultuous South, just where we didn't know and hardly cared, but with the confidence of youth and inexperience we considered ourselves a match for anything we might encounter.

A word of introduction as to who and what we were that sailed away from New York that bright spring morning to put down the Rebellion may be pardoned.

Varian's Battery consisted of six smooth-bore six-pounder brass pieces, with carriages, obtained from the 7th Regiment, and thirty-six horses, all that could be collected in the brief period allowed for that purpose. We were provided with 200 rounds of ammunition per gun.

The *personnel* of the Battery was, perhaps, unexcelled by any organization that ever went into the service. The Captain, Joshua M. Varian, was a very popular officer in militia circles, and held in high esteem by all who knew him. When it became known that he needed a few recruits to bring his company up to a battery standard, some of the best men in the city besieged the armory in their efforts to be enrolled, and it required but an hour or so to obtain all the men that could be carried, while he was obliged to refuse hundreds.

The nucleus of this Battery, "The Gray Troop," was composed of some of the most prominent business men in the city of New York, in fact none were admitted to its ranks except those of good standing in mercantile or professional life, and care was taken that their new associates in the Battery should be young men of creditable antecedents. In the enthusiastic crowd that stood on the deck of the *Montgomery* in the gray light of that April morning were (the subsequently Hon.) Edward Kearney, chief of piece, who distinguished himself not long afterwards by retaking the light-ship at Smith's Point, on the Potomac; Gunner James Lynch, afterwards Sheriff of New York City; Private James S. Fraser, since then Department Commander of the New York G. A. R., and numerous other privates who were to wear officer's bars and eagles before the war was over.

When the steamer cast off her moorings and swung out into the channel, Captain Varian, standing on the upper deck, proposed three cheers for the flag floating over us, three for our beloved New York, and three more for the dear ones we were leaving behind. When the last was given it is no blot on their manhood to state that not a few turned aside to conceal the tears that welled into their eyes. But the voyage had begun, a new and probably stormy phase of life was unfolding, and the path to a glorious career seemed shimmering before us on the dancing waves glistening in the first rays of the rising sun.

After passing Sandy Hook it was ascertained that the ship was bound for Annapolis, Md. All went smoothly until the 21st, when an incident occurred which has not yet found a place in history. It had been rumored that more than one cruiser carrying the Confederate flag had caused considerable damage to Federal vessels, and many hasty glances were cast towards the two guns in the bow while the boys discussed the probabilities of falling in with one of these unwelcome customers. So it is not to be wondered at that a cry from the lookout at the mast-head of "Sail Ho!" caused every man to rush forward, eagerly scanning the surface of the ocean in the direction indicated, and long before they obtained a sight of the vessel signaled, it is safe to say she was secretly considered by every one as something *suspicious*. Finally, when she hove in sight, this belief was confirmed, for it would have been difficult to find a more rakish looking craft. Instinctively each man moved nearer to the guns. Captain Varian stood near the wheel-house, while the captain of the ship, with glass and trumpet, stood by to execute any orders given. Somehow, by the time the vessels were within hailing distance, the men had crept up to the guns and stood ready to open fire. All eyes were closely watching the approaching piratical looking craft, which was about to pass us on the starboard side. What a mean, skulking thing she appeared to be! Now the moment to challenge was at hand, and the captain of the *Montgomery* hailed the mysterious stranger, demanding her destination, whence she came, etc. Of this modest request not the slightest notice was taken; then the notion got into the boys' heads that she was trying to slip away, after having discovered our guns and the resolute men ready to serve them, but Captain Varian was equal to the occasion and at once gave the order to load with a solid shot and fire across her bows. (This means "heave to or take the consequences"; it is, in fact, an insult, and if not heeded in time of war, the vessel firing the shot should, in accordance with the custom of the sea, at once open fire with a view to cripple or sink her adversary.) Away sped the old six-pound ball, ricocheting in front of this insolent cruiser who had disregarded the invitation to explain her presence, but before the smoke had cleared away some one, after the style of gazers at a Fourth of July fire-works display, exclaimed, "Ah! Ah!" This caused others to look, and there, within five hundred yards was discovered a sight that chilled our blood. The port-holes of this strange craft were open and from each protruded the muzzle of a long, nasty-looking gun, manned by "Uncle Sam's" Marines, ready to give us a broadside which would, in all probability, have sent us to the bottom. Then in thunder tones came the command: "Send an officer on board, d——d quick." This, it is needless to say, was done without unnecessary delay. Explanations followed, and it was gratifying to know that "Varian's Battery" had taken a prominent part in the first naval engagement after the fall of Sumter, and had brought-to the *Grape-shot*, U. S. M. Service, whose commander condescended to say that he judged it was a lot of militia or he would have sunk the outfit. As he sheered off he kindly volunteered this piece of information: "The next time you wish to hail a vessel, fire a blank, or you may not get off so easily."

CHAPTER II

In Camp at Annapolis—A Tilt with General Butler

AFTER quite a tedious sail around Cape Henry and up the Chesapeake Bay, we arrived at Annapolis, Md., about noon of the 22d of April, where Captain Varian reported to General Butler, then in command of the post. He directed that the Battery be disembarked and parked inside the marine grounds. This was accomplished after a good deal of hard work. We lacked, however, a complement of horses and harness. Providence furnished the horses in a curious way, which I will now relate, but it took the United States Government some time to provide the harness.

During a severe storm one night over one hundred horses were lowered from a steamer outside and swimming ashore were attracted by the whinnying of our thirty-six animals fastened to the picket rope, and at once joined them. The grounds being enclosed by a wall on three sides rendered it easy to capture and tie up the entire lot. They were turned over to the Government at Centreville later on. General Butler, with that restless energy characteristic of him, ordered two detachments of sixteen of our men each, to be instructed in handling two thirty-two pounders stationed in Fort Severn and used formerly by the marines for practicing. The commander of the brig *Perry*, at anchor near by, kindly consented to give instructions, and loaned our officers a book on naval tactics. The preliminary drill requires each man from No. 1, to 16, inclusive, to "speak a piece," *i. e.*, when the gun's crew has taken its position, at the command of the officer in charge to "cast loose and procure," then No. 1 explains his duties, followed by No. 2, and so on to the end.

I was assigned to the command of these detachments and reported to our naval instructor in the Fort, who, after explaining some minor details, produced the book and remarking that it would take some time to post the men, promised to call around the next day.

I hit upon a plan that enabled us to make a good showing in the morning, viz. : I copied on separate slips of paper each man's "piece," so that all could study at the same time, and during rehearsal that afternoon succeeded in making our drill a perfect success. We were at it again early the next day, to make assurance doubly sure, and when the naval gentlemen put in an appearance we were carelessly lounging around the drill room. I think it was one of the proudest moments of my life when I called the men to quarters and sang out "Cast loose and procure." The boys were prompt and rattled off their pieces without one mistake. The guns were loaded (in our minds) and run out ready for discharging ; meanwhile our instructor looked on in astonishment, declaring it required one year's time and several marlin spikes to accomplish on board ship what we had mastered in twenty-four hours.

We felt very proud of this work, especially when there appeared to be some grounds for the rumor that the enemy intended to make us a visit by water.

Shortly after this I had the ill-luck to come into personal collision with General Butler, through no fault of mine, in a way that is amusing enough to recall now, but which did not strike me that way at the time of its occurrence. I had a spirited gray horse which I was accustomed to ride outside the walls, in company with the other Battery officers, every evening when not on duty. The horse was a famous jumper and as I felt quite proud of his abilities in that line I was always on the lookout for a fence to put him at and show off his steeple-chasing qualities. As we frequently met the General and his staff out riding, I suppose he noticed the gray's superb action, and so I heard from him.

One evening the Captain sent for me, and upon reporting, he informed me that General Butler wanted my horse. I laughed at this, supposing it was a joke, but when the orderly who had brought the message turned to me and stolidly repeated it, I ceased laughing. The situation was becoming serious. At that time we still retained a large amount of "militia-ism" and were not much disturbed by the commanding tones of ranking officers who, we suspected, had little if any advantage over us in the knowledge of military matters. Still, I concluded it might be as well for me to make a call on the General. I had about made up my mind to do so, when the same orderly, who had delivered the message and returned to headquarters, appeared again and with a salute informed me that the General wished to see me at once.

I lost no time in obeying the order. I found the commanding officer pacing his room in slippers and dressing gown and evidently in very bad humor. I saluted and waited his pleasure. He looked at me with an angry frown for a few moments and then burst out with:

"Are you Lieutenant Smith?"

"At your service, General," I replied, with as calm a demeanor as I could assume.

"Why did you not deliver that horse to my orderly, sir, as directed?" was the next question, in imperious tones.

"Well, General," I answered, with a rather feeble attempt at a smile, "the horse is not for sale; still, if you are particularly desirous of having him, about four hundred dollars might, perhaps, induce me to part with him—to you."

Now this was, probably, a rather free way for a subordinate to reply to his commanding officer, but I was nettled by his dictatorial manner, and I really can not see what else I could have said under the circumstances.

The General stared at me with such a malevolent look out of his good eye that I began to feel quite uncomfortable until, with something very like a grunt, he turned away, and I lost no time in getting out, supposing that was the end of the matter. But I changed my ideas on that point before the sun had set.

The General kept an old tub of a steamer within call for special duty purposes. It was deemed advisable at this time to place a section of guns on board, with two detachments under command of a commissioned officer, for police duty on the bay; it was further ordered that neither the officer nor men should land without permission from the General commanding. Usually an order of this kind would have directed the Captain of the Battery to detail an officer, etc., but judge of my surprise to learn that the General had directed that "Lieutenant Smith and one section of the Battery" be detailed for this duty. Practically I had no command, being the lowest ranking officer in the company, and to comply with the order some one would be deprived of his section. However, on board I bundled, not without making a gentle "kick," believing I was the victim of persecution. There was no way out of it but to take my medicine. For two weeks we cruised up and down the bay, during which period the General came on board with his staff for a trip to Fort McHenry. The day was very warm, as I had good reason to remember. Our guns were stationed in the bow without the slightest shelter and, as bad luck would have it, the General took a seat in the wheel-house to make observations. How he managed to twist his eyes in the direction of the guns is more than I can tell ; nevertheless, he did ; then he took a great interest in the practice of artillery, for the time being, and made a pressing request that for his edification the men be drilled. For over one hour we stood under a broiling sun, which did not increase our love for the old man at that time.

Our release from police duty on the bay finally came, when the General took his departure for Fortress Monroe, to which point we escorted him.

EDWARD KEARNEY.

We were ordered to anchor in the "Roads" after our arrival, and not to visit the shore. I think we were detained four days. At last one night at midnight an orderly delivered to me an order to report back to Annapolis. The news was passed and the boys landed the anchor on record time. I stood by the helm determined not to notice anything in the shape of signals, fearing our order would be countermanded. I have always thought there was a little desire to punish me in all this, but it may have been accidental.

While this was going on, another section of the Battery performed very valuable service in securing a light-ship which had been run up a creek to deceive vessels in the night. Of this incident I can say but little, but I remember that Ed. Kearney, then chief of piece, was the hero of this encounter. He boldly stood by his gun and was the only Federal in sight for a brief period. His example and cool judgment, with a little vigorous persuasion added, succeeded in establishing order and turning defeat into victory. A reference to the records as published in the Adjutant-General's Report, State of New York, Vol. I, 1868, a copy of which is herewith appended, will furnish a full account of this affair. See Report, page 169.)

CHAPTER III

On Picket in Virginia—Cub Run—Home Again

THE Battery finally reached Arlington, Va., late in May, 1861, and every night at least one section was posted for picket duty on one of the roads leading from the interior of Virginia.

The night of the great false alarm that brought the army over the Long Bridge from Washington to the Virginia side, I was in charge of two guns on the Vienna Pike. Captain Brackett of the Second Dragoons, U. S. Cav., detailed a sergeant and six men to report to me for vidette and other duty.

About one o'clock A. M. I heard the clatter of a horse's feet coming down the road at a slashing pace, and as he came near the infantry picket a challenge, quickly followed by the report of his piece, ringing clear and loud on the midnight air; still on came the horse. Bang! went another gun, and by this time the frightened beast was panting and blowing among the horses of my section.

It was my duty to investigate and report at once to

General McDowell at the Arlington House. I found that the advanced vidette had dismounted, and relying upon the friendship existing between himself and horse, allowed him to crop the grass. The ungrateful beast evidently intended to play his rider a trick, and watching his opportunity jumped and started for camp. While running the gauntlet one bullet cut him across the crupper, but ere the reports of the guns had died away, it seemed as if every drum on the Virginia side of the Potomac was trying to wake the dead. The long roll was sounded in every camp and was taken up on the Washington side and kept up till the forces in the city crossed over into Virginia, where they formed in line of battle and remained until daylight.

I suppose it took longer to promulgate orders in the earlier days of the war, which may account for the seeming delay in giving notice of the cause, but this was the last of the false alarms in this vicinity. Next day General McDowell issued orders that thereafter no notice would be taken of the discharge of small arms, that the approach of the enemy would be designated by the discharge of field pieces, and officers in charge of such guns were instructed not to fire until they had observed the enemy, with an additional caution that they would be held personally responsible, etc.

Some time in June, while eating our mid-day meal in our pleasant quarters at the foot of the eastern slope of Arlington Hill, an order came from General McDowell to send a section to report to General Tyler, then stationed at Falls Church, Va. We had no idea of the distance or location, but the order stated that a guide would be furnished to pilot the way, and that haste was necessary, as this point was threatened by the "Blackhorse Cavalry."

General Tyler was without artillery, hence much depended on prompt action. The Captain left his seat at the table with the order in his hand and coming to my chair, stopped and asked, "Who shall I send with this section?" having read aloud the order. There was no response; indeed, there could be none until the selection of the section had been announced, then as each section had a commander there would be no question as to who would or ought to go. I was still minus a section and yet felt that I was doomed. It may have been instinct; be that as it may, I was not much surprised when the Captain laid his hand on my shoulder and exclaimed, "You go!"

My first thought was that danger was apprehended and I was made the scapegoat. My indignation almost mastered me, but I left the table saying, "Which section shall I take, sir?" Receiving my answer, I at once assumed command and made speedy preparation for our departure. Many men belonging to other sections honored me by their earnest requests to join the party. Some of them who appealed to the Captain were allowed to do so. My anger was so great I determined to get away without bidding the Captain "Good-bye." Therefore I hastened up the hill after the carriages at a full gallop, but on reaching the summit I found this grand little man shaking hands with the boys. I checked my horse before him, he grasped me by the hand, one look into his eyes and the story was told without one word from either.

It was now about 3 o'clock P. M., and instead of a

guide, a diagram of the route was placed in my hands with a statement that the distance was about fifteen miles. The pace was made accordingly, and if my memory serves me, the first halt made to inquire the way was at "Taylor's Inn," General Tyler's headquarters, less than five miles from Arlington.

In this manner I had the honor of *leading the first artillery from the defences of Washington into Virginia in 1861*, before the grand advance, as well as firing the first shot, which opened the campaign. (See Report, S. N. Y.)

In a few days the balance of the Battery joined us and again I was a free lance.

The services rendered by the Battery while stationed at Falls Church can not be estimated too highly. Constant picket duty on the various roads greatly assisted General Tyler in keeping a clear front.

When the advance began July 14, 1861, Tyler's brigade was assigned to General E. D. Keyes's Division. The Battery had the right of the line for four days, when the head of the Division reached a point near the Fairfax road. Marching parallel to this the enemy were plainly seen moving in the direction of Centreville; their flank being exposed, the Battery took advantage of the situation and opened fire. (See Adjutant-General's Report.) The army was detained by the felled trees thrown across the road, and the Engineer Corps was kept busy in clearing a passage.

A representative of the New York *Evening Express* and myself passed to the front on the Germantown road, riding rapidly until we reached an abatis of felled timber, which my horse managed to pass. Observing a fire and kettle on a tripod, I soon had a nice boiled chicken which the Confederate outpost had hastily abandoned. I also found a felt blanket which served as a cloak or circular by using a cord to contract one end. This I presented to the newspaper man. We then discovered that the enemy had fired some buildings in Germantown. Ayers' U. S. Battery by this time reached the obstructions and to pass the time while waiting for the trees to be removed, threw a few shot in the direction of the enemy.

Afterwards I rode forward to the town, dismounted in front of and entered a large frame house, then burning. The first room visited on the ground floor contained a bed and a few small pictures on the walls; a hasty glance under the bed disclosed a demijohn, which I captured and secured, and with this my curiosity was satisfied. I sat down, carefully guarding my prisoner, when a cloud of dust down the road denoted the approach of a body of cavalry. Up dashed the gallant Tompkins of Fairfax Court-House fame. I knew him well, and followed his troop until a halt was made; then, boldly riding into camp with my prize it goes without saying, my presence was welcomed.

The history of the demijohn was soon told. The burning building had been used as an hospital by the Confederates and my jug contained about one gallon of good medicine, but was it poisoned? The problem was soon solved by Charlie Tompkins who, after smelling, sampled it. Dr. Wilson was horrified, and shouted "Hold on, Lieutenant, it may be poisoned; let me analyze it." "I do n't care, it's d——d good poison anyhow," was the reply. The Doctor, turning to me, remarked, "If Charlie lives ten minutes, we'll try some." Charlie lived.

On the 18th of July our Brigade, which included, among others, the 69th New York, being on the march toward Centreville, had halted in a strip of woods about three-quarters of a mile from Cub Run. General Tyler had gone forward to feel his way to the Run. It was a warm, clear day and we were lounging about in the welcome shade, when we were startled by a sharp roll of musketry from the front. We knew at once that Tyler had developed the enemy and were instantly on the alert. Drivers sprang to their horses, cannoneers leaped to their places, and when an aid came galloping back with a message to General Keyes, we of the Battery felt sure that it meant us. But it did n't. The only troops called for were the 69th. When they received the order to go in they burst into frantic cheering and in a few moments went past us on the double-quick still shouting, and intensely eager to get to the front. The wild excitement was contagious, and mounting my horse I followed the column. When they reached a cornfield about half a mile off, the regiment deployed and soon was hotly engaged. I found General Tyler and his staff behind a belt of timber running east and west at the edge of the field. From here we could see the position of the enemy along Cub Run and protected by the thick woods shading both sides of the stream, about 1,000 yards to the south. Their lines were completely hidden by the trees, affording them excellent cover, while the growing corn made a very indifferent screen for our men. But they fought gallantly until the enemy opened on them from several masked batteries, when they were ordered to retire. As they fell back the Confederate artillery kept up the cannonade, and as they were passing the spot where General Tyler was sitting on his horse the shells kept pace with them, but at an elevation that swept the trees overhead, from which a shower of broken limbs and branches tumbled down on him and his staff. When the 69th came by with gallant Colonel Corcoran and knightly Maj. Thomas Francis Meagher at its head, I rejoined them and returned to the Brigade. I never could understand why our Battery, idly standing within call, was not ordered up to assist the infantry.

In this affair I saw for the first time dead, dying and wounded soldiers, and I remember what a thrill came over me as I noticed a young fellow, his blue uniform stained with his blood, lying dead amid the rows of corn, staring at the sky with sightless eyes—mustered out forever at the very threshold of the mighty struggle. And then how curiously and even admiringly we stared at the first wounded man that hobbled along to the rear in search of medical treatment. I felt like taking off my hat to him. "There," I said to myself, "that fellow will be a hero when he gets home." But we got pretty well hardened to these things before the year was out.

This was the "baptism of fire" for the 69th, and they bore themselves as bravely as ever did their ancestors at Fontenoy, and here they first earned the title that has clung to the regiment for thirty years, "The Gallant Sixty-ninth," a title which was sealed to them by their immortal valor at Bull Run three days afterwards.

After this engagement we were marched to Centreville and there went into camp. Our term of enlistment had expired on the 17th and the question of our discharge was now being agitated, and it became the subject of much and heated discussion. From the drift and general tenor of the discussion it became evident to me that an application for our muster out would be sent in. I was not in harmony with this movement, not caring to leave the field at this time; and made an effort to find an opening where my services might be acceptable. Lieutenant Gordon, of the 2d Dragoons, aide to General Keyes, thought that he could arrange it so that a place on Keyes's staff would be made for me. This was entirely satisfactory, so, to avoid any ill-feeling, as the majority if not all the other officers of the Battery were in favor of the proposed action, I determined to keep away from camp for the day.

In company with Chief of Piece Edward Kearney, a most excellent and companionable young fellow, possessing soldierly qualities of the highest order, I started to visit the battlefield of the 18th. We soon reached the woods where I had seen General Tyler and staff during the fight (having followed the gallant 69th, as related elsewhere). Dismounting, we made our way on foot through the corn field, intending to reach an old log barn which was situated well down and within about 200 yards of Cub Run, where the enemy's pickets were concealed, as we soon discovered.

After leaving the corn field we saw a Confederate hospital flag flying from the roof of a building beyond the stream, but before we could reach the barn several puffs of white smoke down at the Run and the spiteful buzzing of minie-balls in our immediate vicinity admonished us to hug mother earth for safety. Deeming it unadvisable under the circumstances to continue our reconnaissance, having developed the enemy a little too suddenly for our comfort, we retraced our steps, or rather, to state the exact facts, crawled back to the friendly shelter of the growing corn, and so returned to camp without further adventure.

I have frequently since, in recalling this little incident, thought with wonder of the meagre precautions taken in those early days of the war to prevent a surprise. I know we did not see a single Union picket on our trip, although this was the left of our line. It is barely possible that they were in the log barn, but there was no support visible anywhere.

Coming into the large tent, that evening, used by the Captain and his lieutenants, I was informed that a vote had been taken during my absence whether to remain, or to apply for the discharge that was overdue us, and that I was expected to express my wishes. I asked if my vote would change the result, and was answered in the negative. I then declined to vote. "And I, sir," said the Captain sharply, "order you to vote." "Very well," was my answer, "then I wish it to be distinctly understood that I vote to remain."

I don't know whether this decision of mine was expected or not, but it certainly was rather ungraciously received, and the chilly atmosphere of the tent became decidedly unpleasant. So I had my servant prepare me a shelter some distance away, and remove my traps to it. My horse was saddled and picketed near by, and here I awaited with what patience I could muster to hear from General Keyes.

About 10 o'clock P. M. on the 20th, Lieutenant Price, General McDowell's ordnance officer, came into camp and called for the Captain, to whom he delivered an order to turn over the Battery, etc., and take his command to the rear. He then called for Lieutenant Smith. I stepped out and was informed that the Battery was placed in my charge!

This sudden and unlooked for change in the status of affairs took my breath away. The first thought that came to me was this: Captain Varian had been my best and truest friend; I loved and respected him, and I felt that for me to accept this charge would look like a slight to this gallant soldier. Aside from this, lack of confidence in my ability to handle the Battery, and a belief that General Keyes would give me a position on his staff induced me to hesitate. Captain Varian, seeing my embarrassment, suggested that I request a half an hour to consider the matter. During the discussion a number of the men gathered around and intimated that they would stay if I took command. This was very flattering, but I finally concluded that I had better not accept, and so informed Lieutenant Price, and thus I lost the first and best opportunity for promotion that was thrown in my way.

I subsequently learned that this intended honor had been arranged for me through the kind offices of General Keyes, in compliment to my vote to remain.

At 1 o'clock on the morning of the 21st the march to the rear began, and during the tedious tramp to Washington I made up my mind to organize a battery of my own.

And just here it may not be out of place to say a

word as to the action taken by the officers of the Battery, especially as they have been rather severely censured for it. While I did not advocate nor approve the course taken by the company, yet I neither then nor afterward questioned their right to demand their discharge. They had faithfully performed their part of the contract; they had done their whole duty beyond the time for which they were enlisted, and that they should be criticised for simply demanding that the Government should fulfil its obligations to them was rank injustice, and the condemnation of their action contained in General McDowell's official report was unwarranted and ungenerous. Most of the men again enlisted and served in various regiments and batteries. A rather amusing part of the whole affair was that after the application for muster-out was prepared and signed, I, who had voted against it and expected to remain, was selected to present it to General McDowell! He gave me a very cool reception, and after reading it remarked in what I considered an exceedingly rude and abrupt manner:

"Your discharge will be attended to, sir!" and turned his back on me.

From early morn until late in the afternoon the constant booming of cannon served to furnish us food for comment as we marched towards home. In the latter part of the day the cannonading became very irregular, at times being quite rapid, then slackening to a desultory fire. The general opinion was that our army was destroying the enemy.

We reached our old camp at Falls Church that evening and bivouacked there for the night.

By daylight of the 22d, however, abundant evidence of the disaster to our arms appeared. The road from the front was filled with disorganized squads of retreating troops, horses, mules, wagons—all aiming for the Potomac.

But the story of that wild rout has been so often told that its repetition is needless here.

Our company marched in orderly ranks with the mob into Alexandria, which we reached about 3 P. M., and after much trouble secured transportation to Washington that evening. Here we found quarters for the night in a beer garden on Maryland Avenue, and the next morning took train for New York City, where the company was mustered out.

CHAPTER IV

Some Personal Incidents

DURING our stay at Falls Church my duties in camp were light, owing to my position as chief of caissons. This gave me frequent opportunities for scouting on my own hook. On one occasion I suggested to a certain captain of the outpost the rather foolhardy idea of making a raid on the village of Anandale, some four or five miles distant from the advanced picket on the road leading from Falls Church. The officer of the grand rounds was let into the secret and made one of the number selected, he and myself being the only mounted individuals in the party. They all belonged to a Connecticut regiment.

Our plan was to leave a guard with the outpost, and with the reserve (about twenty men, I think) move forward to within half a mile of the village and then divide the force into two equal parts; thus, ten men were to move forward, say one hundred yards, and conceal themselves behind a fence, while the other ten were to remain hidden in the same manner, leaving an interval of one hundred yards between, into which the enemy were to be enticed and captured. The captain and myself were to ride forward to attract attention. In doing so we decided (between ourselves) that it would be best for one to drop behind, and in case the enemy should give chase he was to turn and flee as an indication of weakness, at the first sight of the enemy.

After both, with their pursuers, had passed the first ten, they were to blockade the road in rear, when the other ten would throw a line across the front. In this way it was thought to spring a trap that would redound to our glory. My horse being considered the fleetest, it was left to me to raid the town and stir up the "Black-horse Cavalry," said to be camped near by. My arms consisted of a pocket pistol, which was carried in my hand.

Thus equipped and with perfect confidence in our ability to handle forty or fifty of the enemy by reason of the wise (?) disposition of our force, I dashed into the town, but seeing nothing of the enemy, turned to the left and made for a toll-gate, where I interviewed the keeper. He informed me that a regiment of Confederate cavalry had recently been camped in the woods just outside the village, but it was not certain that they were there now, as none had been seen for a day or two.

I did not make the haste expected of me by the rear guard; at all events on my return I discovered that they had acted upon the principle laid down and advice given by the militia colonel to his troops before engaging the enemy: "Boys," said he, "go in and give them h—l! Fight like the d—l, and if you can't whip them, run!

As I'm a little lame, I'll start now." This proved that

"The best-laid schemes o' mice and men, gang aft agley,"

so the "Black-horse Cavalry" escaped.

I was not quite satisfied with the result of this expedition and resolved to reach Falls Church by a different route from that occupied by the out-post, who had preceded me on the return.

Two or three miles southwest of Falls Church there was a belt of woods extending from north to south, some miles from the Annandale road west. It was composed of small pines standing so closely together that a man could not ride between them on horseback. The soil is very light; at this time it was deep and dusty in the road, which was about wide enough for wagons to pass each other. I determined to reach the western road by the route just described, the distance being about two miles. After having traversed one-half this distance my courage began to weaken. Imagination pictured lurking foes on either side of the lonely road, still there appeared to be no more danger in going forward than in returning so, almost in despair, I sank the spurs deep into the flanks of my willing horse, who sprang forward at the top of his speed, raising a cloud of dust which was observed by Professor Lowe (then located at General Tyler's Headquarters), who had just made a balloon ascension. It was reported to the General, who at once ordered Lieut. Chas. H. Tompkins with "B" Company, Second U. S Cavalry, to find out the cause. Meantime I succeeded in reaching a point where the roads intersected. Here I ran into one of our outposts consisting of three men. I was halted and requested to give the password. This I did n't know, so after a little parleying they placed me in charge of one of their number, at my request, and marched me to the lieutenant in charge of the reserve. Here I found matters in a state of wild excitement caused by the capture a little while before of their captain, who had gallantly offered his services as escort to two young ladies (the Misses Scott) to their home, a few hundred yards distant on a road leading to the northwest and in the open beyond the belt of woods described above.

I satisfied the lieutenant of my identity and started for camp, feeling a little "sheepish" at this outcome to my elaborately-planned raid, but had not proceeded far when Lieutenant Tompkins with sixty men came thundering along. I wheeled, and riding up to the Lieutenant's side soon ascertained that he was after the party responsible for "that dust." I did n't deem it necessary to tell him what I knew of it, and Tompkins branched off toward the Scott house, believing that the party who had captured the captain had also created the dust.

That night and part of the day following was consumed in scouting, ending with the arrest of the Misses Scott and bringing them to headquarters, when, after being questioned by the General, they were allowed to return home.

I kept that dust business to myself, fearing it would cause more strict orders in relation to my privileges.

Previous to this affair there resided in the village of Falls Church an elderly lady with a son and daughter. For some reason the General commanding considered the family as "suspicious" and placed restrictions upon the inmates of the house, forbidding them to leave the premises. The advanced picket line at this time on the road leading to Vienna, and which passed the house occupied by this lady, did not extend as far as the house by two or three rods; the pickets stationed here were instructed to keep a close watch on any visitors and prevent any such from entering the house.

During one of my outings I chanced to reach this station, and while coaxing the picket to let me ride forward up the road for a mile or two (I had no password), I noticed a young lady standing at the gate. After being cautioned by the guard, I was allowed to pass. Her manner plainly indicated a desire to speak to me as I rode by the gate. So stopping my horse I bowed, and she informed me that her mother was very anxious to get a letter to General Scott; that they were nearly starved by the cruel treatment which General Tyler's suspicions had imposed upon them. "Why," said this beautiful, earnest little lady, with tears sparkling like dew-drops in a pair of lovely, innocent eyes, "General Scott rents my mother's house in the city and we came out here for the summer." I said, "write your letter to General Scott and place it on top of the gate post, I will ride forward and on my return will take it, and promise that it shall reach its destination."

I can see her now, although three decades have gone rumbling down the corridors of time, with tears rolling down her sweet face as she thanked me. "If you are ever wounded or sick, or need a nurse," said she, "let me know and I will gladly come." Her deep sense of gratitude and tender years will plead her excuse, if she needs one. Each word sank deep into my heart, I knew her meaning and honored the noble little lady for her sentiments.

That letter reached General Scott, and the very next day a carriage and passes came from the city, to which this persecuted little family returned. As they passed headquarters and the Battery's camp I was inquired for, but as usual was out of camp. They left with the Captain their expressions of gratitude for me.

Upon my return a message from General Tyler to report at once, caused me to apprehend a rating for leaving camp without permission, but I was rather astounded when he abruptly broke out with—

"Lieutenant Smith, I am informed that you are aiding suspicious persons to escape to Washington." I boldly declared that I had mailed a letter addressed to General Scott, and if that was aiding in the escape of suspicious persons, I was ready for punishment. This ended the matter.

On another occasion I arranged with a countryman who brought vegetables and berries to our camp, and with whom I had become quite well acquainted, to go out home with him to dinner, and, as he suggested, enjoy a square meal.

His farm was about four miles from the village, on or near the Vienna pike. The day selected for this trip was an extremely warm one, and the road excessively dusty, but I kept bravely on, enduring the sun's hot rays and as we got out of sight of camp, filled with misgivings as to the prudence of venturing so far into what might well be called the enemy's country, my active imagination began to conjure up foes in every bush. I quietly withdrew my trusty pistol from the saddle holster and placed it inside my coat, which I buttoned closely to prevent the pistol from falling.

Arriving at our destination, the view of a lonely farm house, surrounded by thick woods, did not add to my equanimity.

I began to suspect, though utterly without reason, that a trap had been laid for my capture, but could not make up my mind to turn and make a break for camp, as I certainly had not the slightest evidence of any intended treachery.

Passing through a gate I noted the height of the fence, and felt satisfied that my horse could carry me over it, if necessary.

When dismounted my host kindly offered to care for the animal, but to this I positively objected, and left him under the shade of a tree in the yard, where I knew he would be found if not interfered with. He would not allow strangers to touch him, but would always come at my call. I never tied him to anything but the picket rope.

Entering the house, I was politely offered a glass of brandy which I discreetly declined. Dinner was soon on the table and it was a very good, substantial one, which I would have hugely enjoyed under other circumstances, but during the meal the perspiration fairly streamed down my face, but I dared not unbutton my coat, as then the pistol would be exposed.

I managed to keep my back to the wall and my eyes open to all that took place around me. As the dinner progressed my distress increased. I really do n't know how I answered my host's well-meant efforts at conversation, nor how I got through the dinner. I was possessed with an overpowering anxiety to get away as speedily as possible. I believe I finally took my leave by backing out of the house.

Calling my horse I mounted, while trying to devise some plan for a rapid departure that would not expose my suspicions. I felt that it would be impossible for me to ride away quietly with my back towards the people whom I believed to be plotting my destruction.

As my farmer friend started to open the gate that I might pass out, a sudden inspiration came to me and I said:

"Never mind the gate. Just watch my horse take that fence."

Driving the spurs into the animal, now that I had a good excuse for doing so, he rushed at the fence, bounded over it like a deer, and dashed down the lane in a mad gallop which was kept up until we reached the main road. Here, feeling pretty safe, I pulled up and opened my coat to cool off, and soon reached camp.

When my nerves had recovered their tone I felt rather ashamed of myself, and was very glad that none of the boys had seen the dreadful funk I was in.

What opinion the farmer and his family formed of my queer actions I don't know, for I very carefully avoided him thereafter when he was about the camp, and during the rest of our stay in that locality I kept within the lines.

PART II

THE FOURTH NEW YORK BATTERY

Its Formation, its Services, and its Dissolution

CHAPTER I

Organization—On to Washington

RETURNING home after a service of three months in the field, very much dissatisfied with the manner in which my brief military career had terminated, my former resolve to organize a Battery now occupied my whole time and energies.

In the early days of 1861, organizing and equipping companies of light artillery was no small undertaking; the State authorities furnished but little help in the way of information, so that progress in that direction was necessarily pretty slow.

My first intention was to attach the Battery to a

regiment of infantry then being raised by Col. John Cochran, believing it was necessary that batteries should be thus attached. At this time independent batteries had not been heard of, so far as I knew.

On the fifteenth day of August, 1861, I enrolled the first man and sent him over to Staten Island, a rendezvous for State troops, and by September 4th thirty-seven men were mustered into the State service.

The company under State regulations was now entitled to elect a captain and a first lieutenant.

Joseph E. Nairn of New York City, who had served in Varian's Battery, was selected for the latter position and myself for that of Captain.

The men were sent down to Staten Island as soon as they were mustered, and commenced drilling without delay. About this time I learned that Col. E. W. Serrell was raising a regiment of engineers, and as recruiting was not brisk, a proposition to attach the Battery to this organization, which, as represented, would entitle the men to the same pay as that of first-class engineers, was readily accepted by me. Large posters setting forth that authority had been obtained from the War Department by Colonel Serrell to organize a regiment of engineers with a battery attached and all to receive pay as first-class engineers, were furnished me by the regimental organization and used in good faith; and every man who enlisted thereafter in the Battery was informed that while his duty would be that of an artillerist his pay would be the same as that received by the engineer corps, viz.: $17.00 a month (a misapprehension, as shown by the sequel).

Mr. J. Courtland Parker, a young graduate of the

ORGANIZATION.

New York bar and a nephew of Mr. Parrott, enlisted in the company with the understanding that he would be commissioned as second lieutenant, jr., and his uncle, Mr. Parrott, presented six ten-pounder rifled guns, with two hundred rounds of ammunition per piece, to the company, whereupon it was decided to name the organization "The Parrott Battery." After consulting with our generous donor it was arranged to have each gun stamped with this name—after a selection had been made. Mr Parrott insisted that each piece should be thoroughly tested before the stamp was applied. Several guns, I will not undertake to say how many, were transported from the foundry to the target ground. Here one at a time they were mounted and thoroughly tested as to range and accuracy. Three or four days were devoted to this work, when the guns were finally left at the foundry subject to my order.

Recruiting posts were opened at Oswego and Carmel, N. Y., and by October 24th, 1861, one hundred and thirty-six men and five (prospectively) commissioned officers were borne upon the company roll; before this, however, Col. E. W. Serrell left the rendezvous on Staten Island with a part of the regiment and sailed for Port Royal, S. C.

I now relied entirely upon such instructions as were from time to time received from the headquarters of the regiment. Realizing that the date of our departure was near, I applied at regimental headquarters in New York for final instructions and was directed to report to General Marcy in Washington, D. C., who, it was said, understood all the particulars regarding the organization of the Battery and its connection with the regiment, and would have the former forwarded to Port Royal to join the latter. Mr. Parrott was requested to ship the guns to Washington.

Everything being ready by October 24th, I called at the Adjutant-General's Office, State of New York, in Walker Street, to get an order on the Quartermaster-General for transportation. But before I had an opportunity to make known the nature of my business, General Hillhouse called me into his private office and in the presence of my 1st sergeant, E. S. Smith, made the following proposition:

"Captain," said he, "how would you like to have your Battery brigaded with three other companies now on the island? I intend to form a batallion of artillery under the name of 'The Morgan Light Artillery'; you have the largest company and I will commission you a major and give you the command."

I replied, "General, I could not think of it! My men have been enlisted under the impression and promise that they would receive the same pay as first-class engineers, by reason of authority said to have been given to Colonel Serrell by the authorities in Washington. By accepting your proposition it would appear as though I had bettered my position at the expense of the men, who have been enlisted under this inducement."

"Very well," said the General, "I merely mentioned it to you as a matter of courtesy. I propose to do it."

Bidding the General good-day, I took my leave, without asking for the transportation order, and hastened down to the office of Col. D. D. Tompkins, Q. M. G., No. 6 State Street (relying upon a slight acquaintance obtained through an introduction from his son, a

ON TO WASHINGTON. 37

lieutenant in the U. S. Cavalry), to try and obtain transportation for my company to Washington, without an order from the State.

The Colonel promptly complied with my request, saying: "Bring your men here to-morrow and I will have the papers ready."

From here I hastened to the Island and arranged to have all men who were absent notified of our intended departure on the day following. Every man was on hand, and my scheme to run away the command from the State of New York proved highly successful. I felt proud of the achievement, believing I had acted an unselfish part to benefit the men and fulfill the promises made to them. We left Jersey City about 6 P. M., October 25th.

At Philadelphia a committee from the Merchants' and Mechanics' Association met us at midnight and escorted the company to the dining rooms of the association, where a very acceptable and timely repast served by the wives and daughters of said Merchants and Mechanics was highly appreciated by those renegades who were escaping from their State to serve the flag.

At Baltimore some kind persons under the auspices of a few loyal women, I have since learned, furnished coffee to the boys while they were lounging on the platform waiting for cars to carry them to the Capital. Here, after a wearisome delay of several hours, some old cattle cars, reeking with filth, were run up, which we were informed constituted our train. I forbade the men entering, declaring we would march the entire distance on foot before I would consent to have them occupy cars unfit for animals. There was no fun about my kick and I fear my language may have been more vigorous than elegant; be that as it may, it was not very long before decent cars were provided, and the trip to Washington was completed after consuming twenty-six hours en-route.

On the 27th I reported our arrival to General Marcy, explaining the particulars, as he was apparently ignorant of the existence of such an organization as the regiment with a battery attached. He referred me to Gen. B. F. Barry, Chief of Artillery, who at once informed me that it was contrary to orders for mounted troops to be attached to regiments of foot, but advised me to lay the subject before the men, telling them they could not serve as light artillerists and receive pay as first-class engineers, but if they wished he would mount the company as a light battery; otherwise they would be sent to the regiment, but not as a battery. He further said that by consenting to be mounted at that time the men would not be prevented from joining their regiment at some future period, provided Congress passed a law legalizing the attachment of artillery to infantry.

This question was plainly and fully discussed by the men, who, after one or two days consumed in deliberation, decided to accept the proposition to be mounted as a battery of light artillery, reserving the right to join the regiment under the foregoing provisions. All but thirteen men agreed to these terms.

During this time the company was quartered in the "Soldiers' Retreat," but now General Barry issued forage-wagons, and tents, minus poles and pins—the latter were procured from the woods near the Eastern Branch —and we soon were in quarters at "Camp Duncan," East Capitol Hill.

I made an application to General Barry for the six guns forwarded by Mr. Parrott; to my surprise I was informed that the guns had been issued and that I could not have them under any consideration. This was a grievous disappointment and, I then thought, a piece of rank injustice, but the inflexible reins of military discipline were beginning to tighten on us, and objections to orders were futile and dangerous.

We had our first company muster for pay November 1st, made by Captain, now General, Gibbon, U. S. Artillery. Battery "D," N. Y. Light Artillery, was the name given us by General Barry, and a few weeks later it was changed to Battery "C." The officers' commissions were held back by the State authorities, consequently the organization, so far as the State was concerned, was without a name or number. General Barry communicated with the State Adjutant-General, and finally declared unless our commissions were forwarded without delay, he would muster the company as U. S. troops.

In response to this the commissions were received and the organization designated as the 4th New New Independent Battery.

We were actively engaged at Camp Duncan in daily drilling as drivers and cannoneers, dismounted, as there were neither spare horses nor guns in the District We waited with what patience we could, till the Government would be able to supply us.

One day, in the early part of November, I called on General Barry, and, to my surprise, he said, without looking up: "Captain, I am going to break up Battery "C," Chicago Light Artillery, which is near your camp, and have prepared an order for Captain Busteed to turn over to you all ordnance and quartermaster's stores now in his possession; be very careful and inspect the property before receipting for it."

During the delivery of these instructions Captain Busteed himself entered and was a listener to the greater part of General Barry's remarks. Turning in his seat General Barry faced him and at once repeated the substance of the order, which he held in his hand.

Before sunset I was in possession of a complete six-gun battery, composed of four ten-pounder Parrotts and two six-pounder brass field pieces, and one hundred and thirty-two horses. I also secured eight enlisted men, and with a swelling heart I found myself at last the proud commander of a splendidly equipped Battery, ready for duty in the great army gathered at the Capital.

Now we began work in earnest. We were all lamentably deficient in knowledge of our duties, but we possessed the means of informing ourselves, viz.: a book of instructions in artillery tactics, issued by the Government, and we were not too proud to consult it. I never gave an order which I could not explain—if I blundered the men were not censured for it; if requested by an inspecting officer to execute a maneuvre with which I knew the men were not familiar, I would frankly admit that they had not been instructed in that particular movement, and so were not competent to execute it properly.

I speak of this trifling matter because I have seen battery commanders who issued orders during inspection and *on* the drill field, not understanding or being competent to explain the same, and then, assuming to be much annoyed, they would declare that the men of their command were so stupid that it was difficult to beat anything into their thick skulls.

I also have personal knowledge of two captains of batteries who were most righteously discharged by reason of an attempt to thus vilify their men, to hide their own ignorance.

When it happened that the men of my command did not understand matters appertaining to their duties, the fault was mine. I had failed to properly instruct them. I venture the assertion that this reasoning holds good in ninety-nine similar cases out of every hundred.

Before 10 o'clock A. M., November 24, one of General Barry's aides brought me a verbal message that the General would review and inspect the Battery at 4 P. M. We were ready for him when the time arrived, passing in review at a walk and trot without a mishap; after this, inspection, and a talk with the cannoneers to get an idea of their general intelligence. Then the General, turning to me, stated that he had, during his experience, inspected batteries which had been in service as many years as we had weeks, which had not pleased him so much. "Can you," he added, "be ready to march by 5 o'clock to-morrow morning?"

I replied, "Certainly!"

Fortunately, I had a large quantity of hay and grain on hand which would serve us for the march, to which I called his attention. "O, well, you must take it with you," said he, "I will send the wagons in charge of a wagon-master to report to-night. Your destination is Budd's Ferry, lower Maryland, where you will report to General Hooker."

The boys were wild with delight to get a chance to go to the field, and began their preparations at once.

We crossed the Eastern Branch before sunrise on the 25th of November, a cool, crisp morning, and after a pleasant march through the bleak hills of Maryland reached Budd's Ferry at 6 o'clock P. M. on the 28th, and when the bugle sounded "drivers dismount," and a moment later "unhitch and unharness," we went into what proved to be our winter quarters.

It may be noted just here that General Barry's warm praise had the effect of inspiring confidence in the whole company. Park and field drills were zealously practiced during the winter, and the company could execute every maneuvre in the book before our departure on the Peninsula campaign in March, 1862.

CHAPTER II

Winter Quarters in Lower Maryland—Incidents

DURING our stay at Budd's Ferry our time was principally occupied in performing picket duty opposite Shipping Point battery. The enemy had captured the old river steamboat *George Page*, and kept her behind a small strip of land, in one of the streams which enter the Potomac at this point, for the purpose of securing any vessels that might be disabled by their batteries.

To offset this, General Hooker caused a hole to be dug on the edge of the river bank near the "Budd" house (directly opposite the outlet to the stream in which the *Page* was stationed), large enough for two field pieces. Planks were laid for the gun carriages to rest on, to enable the gunners to make some calculation as to range and elevation. Here one section of artillery was constantly stationed during the blockade, to counteract and prevent the *Page* from interfering with Union vessels, should occasion arise.

It is needless to say that she did not leave her moorings once while the blockade lasted, and was burned by the enemy when it was raised.

This picket duty offered an excellent opportunity for practice in gunnery. A perfect range of the works across the river was obtained, and we soon became quite expert in placing our shots just about where we wished. On more than one occasion have I driven the sentry from the parapet by the accuracy of the aim; the distance was, I think, about two thousand yards, and our annoyance was so great to the enemy, at times, that they would return our fire with an apparent determination to annihilate us. Sometimes the large shells would nearly fill with sand the hole we occupied, but they could not put a shot into it, at least, they did not.

During these spasmodic attacks we would hug the bottom of the pit, and when their fire ceased we would open up and tantalize them again. Reliefs took place under cover of night, leaving the carriages in rear of the "Budd" house during the day.

I remember visiting this post one night; the moon was shining brightly and it was expected there would be some fun, for there was little doubt but some enterprising Yankee skipper would try to run the blockade. We were not disappointed, for at one time white sails appeared to cover the surface of the water as far as the eye could reach, all going up stream. They sailed very near the Maryland shore, while the channel is on the other side.

They were, of course, plainly visible from the other side, and the firing from the forts there was very rapid, but no damage was done to any vessel so far as known·

I heard one fellow sing out, "Fire away, you pesky cusses, you can't hit anything"; and each time a shot would pass over or go near his schooner he would yell and ridicule the inaccuracy of the enemy's aim. At last a shot passed through one of his sails, which seemed to paralyze him for a moment, but recovering his voice he shouted to his fellow sailors, "I'll be d——d if they did n't put a shot through my sail." After that he kept silent.

While we lay here the famous passage of the *Pensacola* occurred, now a matter of history. We had been informed of her coming and consequently were on the *qui vive*. The night was dark and from out the gloom came a low, swishing sound caused by the steam being nearly shut off, I presume; but we heard the sound before we could see her. Great anxiety prevailed among those present as to the success of the passage. Scarcely a word was spoken, while the cannonading was very heavy from all the enemy's works. It did not seem possible that a ship of her size could escape "scot" free. No one seemed to hope for this.

The explosion of shells between our shore and the *Pensacola* was appalling; the earth was torn up along the river bank where the shot plunged, giving it the appearance of an ancient potato field after digging time.

We had no means of knowing at the time how much or how little damage was done— we only knew that the dark mass of shadow continued on her course, and that was enough to relieve the terrible strain endured for many minutes.

In this connection I remember that in the winter of

'62-'63, while marching from Manassas to Falmouth, Va., with Hooker's old Division, then under command of Gen. D. E. Sickles, we camped one night at Dumfries, Va., about five miles as the crow flies, from Budd's Ferry, Md. Here we were informed that all the gunners who participated in the bombardment of the *Pensacola* were imprisoned by the Confederates for their failure to cripple her. And in this same town I saw a solid Parrott shot which one of the citizens had picked up in the street the preceding winter and kept as a relic. I was informed that this shot had been fired from Budd's Ferry, Md. The 4th New York Battery had the only Parrott guns stationed at this post during the period the shot was said to have been fired. I was surprised to learn that a projectile could be propelled through the air so great a distance by these guns.

The first winter of our military career was passed in lower Maryland on Mr. Posey's farm, our camp being about a mile back from the river. General Hooker advised Mr. Posey to collect his rails and pile them near his house, and he (General Hooker) would have a guard placed over them.

This was done but, in some manner never explained, the rails were not to be found in the spring. Several paths leading from the spot once occupied by the rail pile were visible to the naked eye, but alas the rails had vanished. How the guards accounted for the total disappearance of their charge I do not know. The First Mass. Volunteers, Battery "H"; 1st U. S. Artillery, Battery "D"; 1st New York, and Smith's Battery were all located on this farm.

One fact worthy of mention is that Mr. Posey had

not made friends with the boys. For instance, at the time we located on his premises some of the men found two sucking pigs, very small, which they took to their cabins and fed on condensed milk with a spoon until old enough to eat other food. These pigs became great pets, and when old enough followed the horses to and from water and would show fight if a horse refused to let them have a share of oats or corn while feeding. When half grown one was kicked to death by a horse; the other, black as coal, roamed at will, rigged out in a cover made from a scarlet saddle blanket.

I frequently received reports from the 1st Mass. camp concerning the conduct of his pig-ship, whose freedom in officers' quarters was the talk of the camp. He stoutly resisted any attempt to remove him. Mr. Posey heard that we had a shoat in camp and straightway put in a claim of ownership, which could not be well denied, as the animal was found on the premises. But we knew the pig owed his life to the care and attention of those who had raised him.

These facts were laid before Mr. Posey when he came with two slaves to assist him in taking possession. He, however, refused to argue the matter, and armed with authority from General Hooker demanded that the pig be delivered up. I offered to pay any price he might ask in reason rather than order the men to surrender their pet. His only reply was, "I want my property."

"Go and take it," I answered finally. He told his slaves how to proceed, and the boys of the Battery, who fully understood my sentiments, were not slow in devising a way to solve the problem and settle the difficulty.

They at once offered to help catch the object of all this contention, so about fifty men started in hot pursuit of the pig, managing, however, to keep near the negroes, and whenever one of the latter was in the act of stooping to seize a leg, several men would accidentally rush against and send him heels over head. Mr. Posey after fuming and fretting over the ridiculous spectacle, requested me to order the men away, which I declined to do. It was very evident that the Yankees were going to retain possession for the time being. So hostilities ceased, not to be renewed.

I might add that Mr. Pig lost his life at Hampton, Va., when following the horses to water. He was killed by a New York lancer, who was ignorant of the fact that he was a Battery pet. After some loud talking the matter was disposed of by the men of the Battery dressing and roasting "Pat," whose untimely end was regretted by none more than myself.

Another appendage to the Battery was in the shape of a white bull dog named Chauncey, brought from New York by some member of the company. Chauncey was very useful. He too had a scarlet cover, and while sitting on an ammunition chest during a march, as was his wont, his general appearance was such as to increase one's respect for the canine family. Chauncey was never frolicsome, always sedate and dignified.

The many cabins with green hides stretched over rafters for a roof bore evidence to his skill in catching and holding cattle till they were disposed of without the usual noise made by shooting, a dangerous proceeding where a provost guard was in the neighborhood.

Some people lost cattle in the vicinity of Budd's

Ferry and reported the fact to General Hooker. An investigation followed, and the hides referred to caused the occupants of the cabins so covered to be placed in arrest. A court was in session in Posey's house, and the men were ordered for trial. I felt apprehensive, fearing the evidence was too convincing. Lieut. Parker assured me there was no cause for worriment.

"I am going to defend the boys, and clear them, too," said he.

This statement proved to be correct in the end, but how it was accomplished I never learned.

This recalls another little incident, although it occurred some months later.

In August, 1862, when near Bottom's Bridge, on our retreat from Harrison's Landing, Va., after going into camp one afternoon, Generals Hooker and Heintzelman rode forward to inspect the crossing at the river, when, unexpectedly, four men carrying two sheep emerged from the high corn near the roadside, which had hidden them from view. Too late they discovered the presence of the Generals, so they boldly faced the music.

"Where did you get those sheep?" asked General Hooker, pointing in the direction of a brick house; one of the men replied, "Over there." "Very well," said the General, "take them back, but first give me your names."

This was apparently done and a memorandum made. "Ah!" exclaimed Hooker, "I see, you belong to 'Smith's thieves'" (a nick-name he had given them after the cattle trial; but he used to say, "they have a redeeming quality—they will fight!"); "well, report yourselves in arrest to Captain Smith."

The men started off towards the brick house, while the Generals continued their journey.

Next day, while marching through the dust and heat, I heard some cheering, caused, as I soon learned, by General Hooker and staff riding along our flank to reach the front. He asked one of the staff officers the name of the Battery and sent for me. Riding out from the road I reported.

"Captain," said he, "did four of your men report for the guard-house last night for sheep stealing?"

"No, sir," was my answer; but I thought of the mutton chops enjoyed the night before. He drew from his pocket an old envelope and read off the names of the culprits, as he supposed, which he had written down the day before.

"General," I said, "there must be some mistake; the names you have mentioned are not on my rolls."

He stared at me a moment, while a smile crept over his handsome face; then realizing how he had been duped, he could not resist a broad grin, ending the interview by adding—"The d——d rascals."

CHAPTER III

Yorktown.

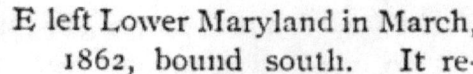E left Lower Maryland in March, 1862, bound south. It required three schooners to transport the horses and the drivers, while the cannoneers and carriages were put on board an old ferry boat.
A part of the expedition was storm-bound at Point Lookout, while the balance went on to Hampton Roads—the schooners, with our horses, included.

After the storm had ceased the vessels that had remained at Point Lookout started for Fortress Monroe, but as we approached the mouth of Cheeseman's Creek a steamer from the fort met the head of the fleet and turned our course up the creek, where we disembarked.

The news of the destruction wrought to vessels anchored in Hampton Roads by the Rebel ram *Merrimac* filled us with alarm for the safety of those who were on the schooners. We plainly heard the booming of the cannon while the terrible conflict raged.

Our suspense during the few days separation which

intervened was intense; not one word could we get in the way of information regarding those who were absent. I feared the worst, believing two-thirds of my men had fallen victims without the means of firing one shot in defense; but the arrival of Lieutenant Nairn with every man and horse caused great rejoicing in our camp. He had marched across country from Hampton.

We now moved up near Yorktown to take part in the siege of that historic place. During our stay here the Battery was in continual active service.

Our last night here was spent on picket duty. To me this was the most trying night I remember. The ground pointed out to me where the Battery was to take position was in front of and about eight hundred yards distant from the famous Red Redoubt, and in front of the Federal battery known as No. 3, on the left of the Union line.

I placed the Battery in the woods near by until night to prevent the enemy from discovering our close proximity. I also caused some dry corn stalks to be removed from the field where we were to take position, to avoid making unnecessary noise by the carriages passing over them. This seemed to be prudent, as the enemy's sharpshooters were known to occupy positions in rear of a cluster of standing chimneys, located nearly midway between the lines, all that was left of some structure which had been given to the flames.

After dark, by moving one carriage at a time, the Battery was finally located as directed by the Division Chief of Artillery, accompanied with instructions to protect Battery No. 3, in the event of a sortie by the enemy. (It was undoubtedly a mistake to place the battery in this exposed position before it was required; it should have been posted in rear of the works.)

On this particular night the Federal commander appeared to have reason to believe that the enemy were intending to make a move, and our army was disposed so as to defend the unfinished works along our front.

The enemy did move, but in another direction from that expected by us. While the Army of the Potomac was preparing to repel an assault upon its front, the Confederates were making tracks towards Williamsburg, after arranging to keep up a continual cannonade from their works for many hours during the night to cover their retreat. This ruse was successful. When the Federals moved forward next morning there was not one Confederate soldier found in the fortifications of Yorktown. This ended the siege of thirty day's duration.

All through this dreadful night we were exposed to this fire, and, unused to such demonstrations, it was our firm conviction that the foe intended to come forth from his lair and give us battle. Hence, every shot, with lighted fuse attached, by which it could be traced, traveling in our direction, was eagerly watched until its destination had been reached. Some fell short, while others passed over us, as good fortune would have it, and notwithstanding the close calls made by some of the many shells fired from mortars and huge guns, we received no damage beyond being frightened half out of our wits.

Just before dawn I withdrew the Battery out of range and awaited results. I had no orders for this movement but acted on my own responsibility.

When it became light enough to see, the Army of the Potomac was found to be in line of battle about eight hundred yards in the rear, thus placing my battery between the two lines. And here occurred an incident that might have had very serious results to all concerned. Captain Griffin, U. S. Artillery, whose battery was in rear of my position, rode forward and ordered me to remove my command, saying he intended to shell the enemy. I informed him that I had received my orders from General Hooker. He said he would fire over our heads if I did not withdraw. I replied, "If you do, I will return the fire." Returning to his Battery he gave the order to load, and I reversed my guns. At this moment one of General Hooker's aides came dashing up and directed me to fall back.

I can not say at this late day what would have been the consequences if Captain Griffin had carried out his threat. Reporting to General Hooker he asked what I was doing out there. I said, "your Chief of Artillery is responsible for the predicament from which you have just extricated me."

"My God!" he muttered, "Can't I find any one to carry out an order intelligently?"

Returning to camp preparations were made for our usual Sunday morning inspection, and a brand new uniform was donned in honor of the occasion; in fact never after, during my service, was I so gorgeously arrayed. Light colored kids, light boots and sky-blue trousers, made up the most conspicuous part of my attire.

I had just commenced inspection when the Chief of Artillery rode into the park and ordered me to pull out at a trot, saying, "Yorktown is evacuated and we are going to pursue the enemy."

I prided myself on promptness, and at once gave the necessary orders, detailing a sergeant and six men to strike camp and follow with camp equipage, etc.

The weather was fine, so I left without an overcoat, expecting everything would be up by night.

Before leaving camp, having started the Battery ahead, I visited the hospital. Here, one of our men, a fine young fellow, named Kilby, appealed to me with tears in his eyes to be taken with us, but the surgeon in charge informed me that his condition was serious, if not dangerous, and that it would be madness to grant his request. Reluctantly I was compelled to refuse. Poor boy, he did not long survive our departure, he died four days later.

Another man (Charlton) who was in the hospital for treatment, with glistening eyes and quivering lips asked to be taken in the ambulance. The surgeon not objecting, I consented.

These matters do not appear to contain much of interest to the general public; there is, however, a sequel which will explain the motive for entering into details as to my dress and the hospital episode as to Charlton.

Hastening on I overtook the command before entering the works at Yorktown. Here the advance column of the army seemed to meet with some obstacle. Later on we learned that buried torpedoes were scattered promiscuously in the works around the guns left mounted on the parapets; in fact, some of our troops had been killed by the explosion of concealed shells, before the necessary warning could be given. After this, every foot of the road over which we marched was carefully inspected by experienced engineers, who found many shells buried along the entire route, leaving a small wire exposed two or three inches above the ground, which, being struck by the foot of man or beast would cause an explosion.

The engineers marked the location of these shells by sticking into the ground by the side of the wire a small branch eighteen or twenty inches high, with a piece of colored cloth fastened at the top. (This refers to hidden torpedoes along each side of the road; those that were buried in the middle of the road were removed.)

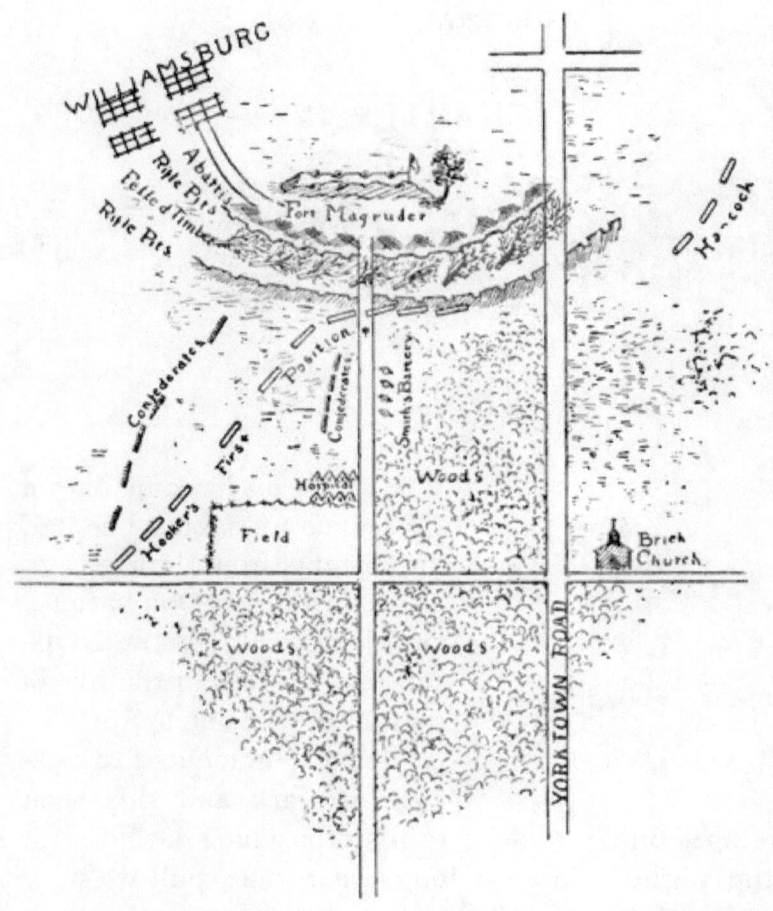

PLAN OF THE BATTLE OF WILLIAMSBURG. FROM SKETCH MADE BY THE AUTHOR AT THE TIME.

CHAPTER IV

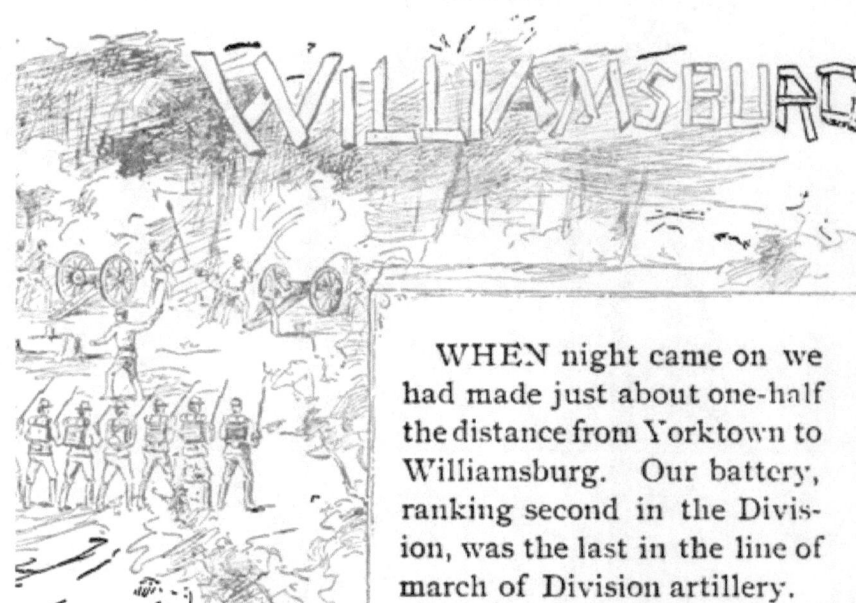
WILLIAMSBURG.

WHEN night came on we had made just about one-half the distance from Yorktown to Williamsburg. Our battery, ranking second in the Division, was the last in the line of march of Division artillery.

It had commenced to drizzle at dark and this soon developed into a violent rain storm which lasted most of the night. After a long, wearisome pull we were halted in front of a brick church, subsequently made famous as a prominent point in the line of march, and remained there in the darkness and rain until midnight, awaiting orders.

The Battery was then moved into an adjacent field and the men were allowed to obtain such rest as they could. With the aid of the tarpaulins they managed to construct fairly comfortable shelters. I had a rather cheerless time, principally owing to the absence of my overcoat, which I had rather thoughtlessly left behind with the baggage.

But the longest night has an ending and at daylight we swung out on the road again and took our place in the marching column, without a mouthful of food for man or beast.

At 6 A. M., sharp firing in front gave notice that the enemy had made a stand.

The Battery, notwithstanding the horrible roads, moved forward, until it reached a cross road, near the church above alluded to. Here we found a forage train mired in the mud and blockading the road. The only way to get by was to cut a passage through the woods, which I decided to do, and the axes of the Battery were at once set in motion by the men, who were wet to the skin, cold and hungry, but willing and anxious to do their whole duty.

While they were thus engaged I rode forward to report the situation to General Hooker. I found him in front of Fort Magruder just in the rear of Battery "H," First U. S. Artillery, and Bramhall's 6th New York Independent Battery, which were posted near the edge of the felled timber, and vigorously engaged.

I stated our condition to him and the difficulty experienced in getting through. Without turning his eager gaze from the front he said quietly:

"Well, Captain, I do n't think you 'll be needed, but get up as soon as possible."

Returning, I found the roads almost impassable, teams being doubled every few rods to extricate gun-carriages from the mud holes, while horses, wagons and men seemed mixed up in irretrievable confusion.

By noon a road, or rather a passageway, had been cut through the dense woods for half a mile, and by vigorous exertion, and, I am afraid, much profanity, five of our guns and caissons were got through.

It was now between 1 and 2 o'clock P. M., and General Hooker's lines were fully a mile away. Just as we had got clear of our improvised road I met Lieutenant Abbott, aide to General Hooker, with verbal instructions from the General to hasten forward.

The guns were then passed in front of the caissons, and the drivers ordered to urge the horses with whip and spur. The road we were now on was new and narrow and bore evidence of having been recently opened by cutting away the underbrush and trees through a strip of heavy timber, and was so arranged that the guns of Fort Magruder covered it.

As we were struggling forward I found Capt. Chauncey McKeever, General Heintzelman's Adjutant-General, actively engaged in posting a line of cavalry to check the retreat of disorganized troops whose faces were turned in the wrong direction. When we came up he shouted to me an order to turn my guns upon these "stragglers," though I do n't think that term could properly apply to men who had been fighting since 6 o'clock in the morning. Rightly judging that this was only a ruse of the captain to command the attention of the weary and disheartened soldiers, I disregarded the orders and continued the march, through masses of wounded men, some being assisted by comrades, while others were hobbling along as best they could trying to reach the field hospital. But a more terrible sight to us, about to engage in our first battle, were the numerous dead who lay where they had fallen in the skirmish of the advance in the morning.

The hospital, and, near by, General Heintzelman's headquarters (in the saddle) were passed; two hundred yards further on I found General Hooker in the middle of the road, without an aide or an orderly in sight.

"Where are you going, Captain?" he asked.

"To the front," was my answer.

"My God! There is no front," he exclaimed. "Can you go in battery here?"

The guns were in column of pieces on a narrow road not more than twenty-five feet wide, the carriages sunk to the naves in mud, but at the command "Action front!" after the General had pointed out the direction from which to expect the enemy, the boys promptly and coolly executed the maneuvre, forming a line parallel with the road with two sections, while one howitzer covered the road leading to the fort.

From the muzzles of the four guns to the edge of the wood opposite the distance was not greater than twenty yards, and from this point we looked for an attack.

As many of Hooker's infantry were still somewhere in the woods, we had to exercise great precaution not to fire upon our own men, who were being forced back by the Confederate advance.

The guns were double shotted with canister, the men standing in the position of "Ready." And now came the most trying ordeal to which a soldier can be subjected. Our instructions were not to fire until the enemy came in sight, and if we failed to repulse to spike and surrender. This was made necessary by the condition of the roads. We could neither retreat nor advance, and as the horses were not needed they were sent to the rear, thus relieving fifteen drivers from the expected storm of bullets.

And then, while the men stood to their pieces, straining their eager eyes to pierce the thick brush in front, a dropping fire was opened on us by sharpshooters completely hidden from view, resulting in the killing of one gallant fellow, Robert C. Lowrie—the last man recruited for the Battery, who had joined us at Philadelphia and been mustered in at Washington. He dropped at his gun and was sent to the field hospital, where he died. In another moment brave Corporal Riker tumbled over, mortally wounded, and then Private George Cipperly suddenly fell from his horse, with a sharp cry, and was carried to the rear. In quick succession John B. Johnston and Robert Shaw dropped badly wounded.

This murderous fire from an invisible enemy was a severe trial to men who had never yet been in the front of battle, especially as no defense could be made, but the Battery boys stood to their posts manfully and quietly awaited orders.

The guns occupied a position upon a knoll on the side of, and elevated about three feet above, the road. Near the edge of the bank General Hooker sat upon his horse, calmly watching the progress of affairs, while General Heintzelman had gathered a few musicians and drummers at the field hospital near by, who, under his orders to "Play Hail Columbia and Yankee Doodle and drum like hell," were doing their level best to make up in noise what they lacked in music.

Presently through the underbrush we could see the legs of a mass of men hurriedly getting into line, their bodies and faces being concealed by the leaves and branches, and it was quite evident that they were forming for a charge. Now was the decisive moment, and cautioning the men in a low voice as to what was expected of them, I gave the order "Commence firing!" A sheet of flame, a terrific roar, followed by three more rounds, double shotted with canister, as fast as they could be fired without sponging, and then, enveloped in smoke, we awaited with intense anxiety the result.

It was as gratifying to us as it was disastrous to the enemy. They had been swept away like chaff before the wind, and none were left but the dead and wounded, who littered the ground in front of us.

At our first round General Hooker's horse reared and tumbled over the embankment into the road. I feared that a "rotten shot" had struck him, but it turned out that the sudden report had startled the animal, and before the General, a splendid horseman, could control him he was over the bank, landing his rider in the mud and falling partially on him. Some of the boys rushed to his assistance, but he extricated himself and quickly assuring them that he was not injured, remounted and road away.

The report of our guns had attracted the attention of the watchful enemy in Fort Magruder, and they instantly opened on us, sending their compliments in the shape of six-pound balls during the rest of the day. But their range was poor and they did little damage. We replied to them, besides shelling the woods wherever there were indications that an attempt was being made to re-form their lines.

As before related, I was in full dress uniform, yellow kids, etc., which I had donned for the inspection at Yorktown the day before, when we were so suddenly ordered to the front. My trousers were now torn and my whole suit soiled with the mud and rain, for the skies poured down an incessant shower the whole day, and having neither rubber nor overcoat I know that I must have presented a rather bizarre appearance, especially with the bright yellow kids, which fitted so tightly that I had not taken the time to remove them, so when, during the afternoon, Gen. Phil. Kearney, the most reckless, daring, general officer that the Army of the Potomac ever had, came riding up, in advance of his Division, to the Battery, which presented the only semblance of a line in sight, his quick eye took in the situation at a glance. Briskly dashing up, he halted near me, and looking me over from head to foot, he burst out:

"Well, you're a d——d fine looking peacock! Who the devil are you?"

I laughed, and we were soon exchanging news. After a short conversation he requested me to cease firing until he rode out to the felled timber to get a better view of the situation. I gave the order, and in a moment he was off up the road at full speed, his horse sending a perfect shower of mud in all directions.

He returned in a few minutes and asked me to advance a section of guns to the felled timber in order to shell some infantry that were visible from there, but added:

"Wait until I see you again," and started back to urge forward his troops. He returned with a small detachment which he placed in the woods opposite us, and then hurried up another squad and so soon established his division in a new line. While thus occupied he noticed a lot of soldiers gathering in the vicinity of the Battery, without officers, and in a sharp tone of voice he asked:

"What troops are you?"

"Jersey," was the reply.

"What brigade?"

"Second," was answered.

"Where are your officers?"

"We haven't any," was the rather sullen rejoinder.

"Well!" shouted Phil. "I am a one-armed Jersey son-of-a-gun, follow me! Three cheers!"

And swinging his cap around his head, he succeeded in infusing new life into these weary, worn-out heroes, who had held their ground while a cartridge could be obtained from the boxes of their fallen comrades, then slowly retired until they reached the Battery. But they were too loyal to continue their retrograde movement while there was a show for making a stand, and they followed General Kearney across the road and into the woods with an answering cheer, and without a round of ammunition among them.

He directed me to take my Battery where the men could rest, and then just at sunset, when the rain had ceased and the clouds parted and the whole western horizon was luminous, he led his division to the charge through the gloomy, rain-soaked woods.

It took but a few minutes to reach the enemy, who had watched these preparations and were ready for them.

They encountered a terrible fusilade to which, from scarcity of ammunition, they could make but a feeble reply, and so were forced back, but the cautious Confederates, smarting from their fearful experience of a few moments before, did not follow.

It was now growing late, and the disorganized soldiers belonging to other commands came back to the Battery, not knowing where else to go, I presume. The General ordered them to form in the rear of the guns as a support, which the brave, patient fellows at once did.

As there was no likelihood of any further hostilities during the night, the Battery was collected and the carriages parked in an open field about four hundred yards in rear of the position we had occupied in the morning, and the worn out, half-famished men, who had eaten nothing since the day before, proceeded to make themselves as comfortable as possible for the night. The tarpaulins were utilized to sleep on, while a sort of shed, covered with poles and brush, was put up for the officers in the adjoining woods. In front of this was built a large fire, kept burning during the night by forming five colored servants into reliefs of two hours each. With a rail for a pillow and a saddle blanket for protection from the wet ground, and feet to the fire, we slept the sleep of utter exhaustion on the battle field.

CHAPTER V

Official Reports—Some Misstatements Corrected

MAY 6th opened clear and warm. It was now remembered, with many pangs, that our fast had not been broken since the morning of the 4th. Appearances were not encouraging, but some of the men were mounted and dispatched to search for our wagons and bring up at least some boxes of hard tack if nothing else, and others were sent out to forage in a quiet way.

The officers were not so well provided for in the way of rations as the men, relying, as they were forced to do, upon the commissary, or what could be purchased from the farmers. I managed, however, to capture three hogs and a steer found roaming in the woods, which were hastily butchered and carried into camp.

By this time some hard tack and coffee were brought up, which, together with the meat cooked on spits, furnished a meal which in our exhausted condition seemed fit for a king.

The officers' servants had secured a few eggs, and borrowing coffee and hard tack from the men, we were able to dine several officers whose situation was more deplorable than our own.

Before night we marched into Williamsburg all in good shape. On the route a Confederate soldier was discovered in the southern edge of the woods upon the northern side of which we had fought the day before. He was without arms and we soon had him in charge. He stated that his captain and a comrade were hidden in the woods both badly wounded; that he had left them to obtain food. I directed him to lead the way to his captain, taking several men and a stretcher with us: by a loud shouting we managed to find their location. Some of my men succeeded in climbing a steep hill, reaching the captain ahead of me, and to them he had surrendered his sword. As he had on a linen duster and trousers inside of drawers, without any insignia of office in sight, I asked why he sought to hide his rank. He replied that he had heard that we shot all officers captured, and this was his reason.

I returned his sword, gave him refreshment from a canteen, with some hard tack, placed him on the stretcher, as he was too weak to walk, and the boys carried him more than half a mile to the road. The wounded enlisted man was able to walk.

I reported and turned over to General Hooker's provost marshal my prisoners. I think the name of the captain was Ward, belonging to an Alabama regiment, probably the 5th. Before parting he assured me of his sincere belief that they (the Confederates) were fighting their friends instead of their enemies, a belief we entertained from the beginning, but it took four years of hard fighting to convince a majority of the Confederate Army.

Referring to the part taken by the Battery in this battle, with all the lights now before me obtained from the published reports in the Rebellion Records not accessible heretofore, I have reason to regret my failure to make a report at the time.

Not being in possession of these facts until their publication, as stated, it was impossible to make an earlier correction of some misleading statements made at the time. General Hooker handed me a copy of his official report while the Division was in camp near Bottom Bridge, and asked my opinion of that part referring to the Battery. I thought it well enough so far as it went, but said it did not do justice to the service rendered by the men at a critical time, when the Battery was pushed forward to meet the advance of the foe who were flushed with the advantage gained by reason of the Federal infantry running out of ammunition; that the position was considered in the nature of a "forlorn hope," the character of our orders, "to double-shot with canister, and if we did not repulse to spike and surrender," plainly indicated; furthermore, that this check to the enemy enabled General Kearney to establish his lines, thereby contributing in no small degree to the victory which followed.

My disappointment was expressed in a respectful manner, as to the neglect to properly mention the value of the services rendered by the action of the Battery. (For myself the reward was on a par with my deserts.)

To this the General replied, "I could not say more without making it look as if the Division was 'skedaddling.'" The paragraph in the report referring to the Battery is this:

* * * "While this was going on in front, Captain Smith, by a skillful disposition of his Battery, held complete command of the road, which, subsequently, by a few well-directed shots, was turned to good account.''

As before stated, the Battery was placed in position under the General's supervision. Now note the remarks of his Chief of Artillery in his official report, to wit:

"HEADQUARTERS DIVISION ARTILLERY, HOOKER'S DIVISION,
"CAMP NEAR WILLIAMSBURG, *May* 7, 1862.

"*Captain :* I have the honor to lay before the General commanding this Division the following report as to the part taken by the batteries under my command in the battle of the 5th instant:

"Being in rear of the infantry, we camped about 1 o'clock that morning, two batteries about half a mile this side of King's Creek and two the same distance on the other side. By 6 o'clock that morning we were *en route*, Battery "H," 1st U. S. Artillery, Captain Webber, and Battery "D," 1st New York Artillery, Captain Osborn, being in advance; Captain Bramhall's 6th New York Battery about a mile in rear.

"On arriving at the front I at once, by the General's direction, ordered Captain Webber to place his guns in battery — one on the road just at the corner of the felled timber which lay on its left, another some twenty yards in rear of this, and the other four in a field on the right of the road. They were immediately got into position, but while the first section in the road was being unlimbered, Lieut. Chandler P. Eakin was shot down close by my side and Lieut. Horace L. Pike near the second piece, as also two of the privates. The drivers of the limbers taking fright, as also some of the cannoneers, they fell back about a hundred yards to the rear of the pieces. Aided by Captain Webber and 1st Sergeant (William A.) Harn, I tried to urge and drive them forward to their guns, but did not succeed in getting a sufficient number up to open fire. I then went back to Captain Osborn's four-gun Battery which had come up, and called for volunteers to aid in manning these pieces. Every cannoneer at once sprang to the front, and headed by their officers, opened fire from four of Battery "H"'s guns, while at the same time Captain Webber got some fifteen or eighteen of his men at the other two. The rain was falling fast at the time, rendering it impossible to see the exact position of the enemy. Our fire was directed in reply to some pieces on the works about seven hundred yards directly in our front, and at a part of a field battery to our front and left, which appeared to be in the open, but which I have since ascertained was in a sunken redoubt.

"Half an hour later Captain Bramhall came up and I immediately ordered him to take position in the field to the right of the other guns, which he did in a most soldier-like manner. The ground in this field was exceedingly soft and full of stumps, so that he was only able to get five of his guns in battery. Our men soon got the range and distance of the enemy, and in half an hour more silenced their guns entirely. They did not fire from the works in front except occasional shots again, until later in the afternoon, but about 10 o'clock they opened again from the sunken redoubt and from another still farther to the left. Finding that these shots were enfilading some of my pieces, I moved my right wing forward in eschelon, and by noon we had again silenced them so effectually that their next effort to open fire about an hour later was a very weak one.

"My men had now been in the open under fire, not only of the guns we had silenced, but of a very severe fire of the enemy's sharpshooters, for some seven hours, and were greatly fatigued. As all had been quiet for some time, I rode to the rear to hasten up Captain Smith's 4th New York Battery, which had been kept back by the bad roads and the baggage wagons of other divisions. It was while I was absent on this duty that the infantry supporting me abandoned the felled timber on my left, leaving my batteries entirely exposed on that flank. They (the enemy) came upon us over this timber, driving the men from the guns, which were badly mired, and having lost a large number of horses we were unable to bring them off. Captain Bramhall gallantly fought his pieces until the battery on his left was fairly in the hands of the enemy, when, finding that his men were exposed not only to the fire of the advancing foe but also to the return fire of his support on the right he ordered his men to fall back. The enemy keeping possession of a portion of the felled timber on our left prevented any attempt again to work or remove these pieces.

"So soon as I got Captain Smith's Battery up I placed four of his guns in eschelon on a knoll to the right of the road, just within the woods, and loaded with canister, to be ready in case the enemy should attempt to charge down the road. This was done about a half an hour later. When the head of their column had approached to within some one hundred and fifty yards, we opened fire on them and effectually stopped their advance. Directly after this we suffered severely from single men of this column who had taken positions in the felled timber on the line of the road, four or five of the cannoneers falling at the advanced piece until General Kearney furnished me with a company of sharpshooters as a support. After this charge was repelled the battery was not seriously engaged, only firing occasional shells in the direction of the works in front and on our left, which had again opened fire. At sunset, with the General's permission, I withdrew my two remaining batteries, leaving Captain Thompson, Chief of Artillery in Kearney's Division, in charge of the position.

"I regret exceedingly to be obliged to report the loss of four of Battery "H"'s guns and one caisson, which were carried off by the enemy when they had possession. Captain Bramhall's guns were so deeply mired that they did not succeed in moving them. I have also to report the loss of four men killed and two officers and eighteen enlisted men wounded, a full list of which is appended. The enemy carried off forty horses with the guns, and we have as many more left dead in the field, besides a number wounded and missing.

"I have reason to be satisfied with the conduct of my officers generally. Captain Webber, who only joined his command since our arrival at Ship Point, showed great bravery in urging his men to the guns; Lieutenants Eakin and Pike fell well to the front at the first fire of the enemy. Captain Bramhall's conduct was that of an experienced officer, having his men in perfect command, and such as fully sustained his gallantry at Ball's Bluff last October. He was seconded by all his lieutenants and men. Captain Osborn and his lieutenants in this their first engagement gave promise of making brave and efficient officers. I would especially mention among the enlisted men Sergeants Harn and (John) Doran and privates (Daniel) Barry and (Daniel) Conway of Battery "H," and privates (John) Shoemaker and (George O.) Westcott of Battery "D," as having done particularly good service. Captain Osborn's and Captain Smith's Batteries are still in condition for service, Captain Bramhall's lacking horses, and Captain Webber's both horses and pieces. * * *

"(Signed)   C. S. WAINWRIGHT.
"*Major and Division Chief of Artillery.*"

To my mind it is clear that a little prejudice existed somewhere. The loss in killed and wounded in the Division artillery was twenty-four, to wit: Battery "H," 1st U. S. Artillery: killed, two enlisted men; wounded, two officers and six enlisted men. Battery "D," 1st New York: killed, one enlisted man and seven wounded. Fourth New York Battery: one enlisted man killed and five wounded (two dying in hospital). Sixth New York Battery report no casualties.

The reference made to the "four or five men who fell at the advanced pieces," and, "After the charge was repelled the Battery was not seriously engaged, only firing occasional shells in the direction of the works in front and on our left, which had again opened fire," could not be told in a less effective manner if the writer intended to belittle the efforts of the men who actually repulsed the enemy's charge.

The statement as to the distance, viz.: "one hundred and fifty yards," and the direction, "down the road," is at variance with my recollection, and, I believe, the facts.

There was an apparent difference of opinion between Generals Hooker and Kearney regarding an infantry support to the Battery. As a matter of fact, the only support was that improvised by General Kearney alluded to before. His finding the Battery without infantry support may have created the belief that the artillerists had been driven from their guns during a brief cessation of cannonading when there was no enemy in sight. At such times the cannoneers were directed to step back into the woods to avoid exposure to the bullets of a few isolated sharpshooters whose fire could not be returned by the Battery. The absence of an infantry support compelled the adoption of this method as the next best means of protection; but at no time was the fire of our guns discontinued by reason of the close proximity of the enemy in force, nor were the men driven from their pieces; on the contrary, they stood ready to and did defend them at all times.

General Kearney says:

* * * "This duty was performed by officers and men with superior intrepidity, and enabled Major Wainwright of Hooker's Division to collect his artillerists and reopen fire from several pieces." (The artillerists of this Battery were not scattered.)

To this paragraph General Hooker replied in a supplemental report, as follows:

"My attention has been called to that part of Brigadier-General Kearney's official report of the battle of Williamsburg, which states, 'and enabled Major Wainwright of Hooker's Division to collect his artillerists and reopen fire from several pieces,' and I give it my positive and emphatic denial. This statement admits of no application to any battery of mine except Smith's, and I deny that any men of his were driven from their pieces, or that the fire from his battery was suspended from the proximity or fire of the enemy's skirmishers at any time during that day. I request that this statement may be forwarded in order that it may be placed on record with my official report of that battle of the 5th instant."

In this connection a paragraph from the official report of Gen. Grover, U. S. Army, who did not know the name of the battery, but, as the records show, from the time the 4th New York Battery took position, no other battery was engaged in Hooker's or Kearney's Divisions on that field ; hence, little doubt remains as to the identity. He states :

* * * "I then withdrew that regiment entirely from that position to support our retreating forces at the point of the woods, and just in time to unmask the position of the enemy and expose him to a most severe fire of canister from a part of a field battery thrown forward for the purpose of checking the rebel advance; and I think from my own observation, that this battery contributed more toward sustaining our position than anything else that could have been brought to bear in that part of the field."

The 4th New York was the only battery in Hooker's Division whose carriages were in park on the night of the battle.

My motive for alluding to this matter at this late day is to render, in a measure, some justice to the men who nobly earned a fair share of praise so lavishly bestowed in other directions. For instance: Lieut. Joseph E. Nairn, Sergt. Richard Hamblin, Corp'l J. A. Thompson, and privates J. B. Johnson, Robert Shaw, J. S. Fraser, W. H. Riker, Geo. C. Cipperly, R. C. Lowrie, and J. C. Charlton were all conspicuous for their bravery. I am writing from memory and do not intend to reflect upon any member of the Battery, but these men have ever been uppermost in my mind for their gallantry—while others there may be who are honestly entitled to honorable mention, and I feel justified in referring to the above by name, believing there are none who will or can object. Many of my men were absent during the battle with the caissons and horses, and in this manner were attending to their duties.

What more could have been asked of these men? And yet their conduct failed to attract the attention of the gallant Chief of Artillery by whose side they fought, and many fell. An impartial comparison of the facts will place the reputation of the Battery in a more favorable light and the unprejudiced will accord to it the privilege of standing upon an equality with those batteries more in touch with the headquarters of the Division Artillery.

Just before the Battery opened fire and while the rain was pouring down in torrents, Charlton, who had ridden from Yorktown in the ambulance, came to me with coat off and sleeves rolled up and asked for the proper elevation, saying he had loaded a gun and was ready to fire it. He remained with the gun while it was in action, but was not physically able to perform his ordinary duty otherwise; therefore, in consideration of his gallantry he was excused and allowed to ride in the ambulance until his health permitted his return to duty. He never missed a fight where the Battery was engaged.

Lieut. Joseph E. Nairn deserved especial mention for his conduct; he was at his post from first to last, as was Serg't Richard Hamblin, who stood by his piece manfully and aided in handling and firing the same.

John B. Johnston and Robert Shaw were shot down at their posts, while Riker, Lowrie, and Cipperly gave their lives by reason of their devotion to the flag.

Usually there is no difficulty in finding men willing to assist wounded comrades to the rear and the hospital, but to their eternal praise be it said, not one man belonging to the Battery would leave his piece to assist the wounded from the field. Some of them threw a tarpaulin down and lifted their disabled comrades out of the mud and placed them on it and then returned to their guns.

Captain Osborn offered to, and did send some men from his Battery to carry back my wounded.

It is a long time since the incidents above recorded occurred, and I am writing without the assistance of notes; many events doubtless have passed out of my mind, but at this moment another incident comes up from the recesses of my brain which I will relate.

When General Kearney requested a section to be sent to the front, the horses were ordered up and everything made ready to carry out his orders. While limbering up, a solid shot from Fort Magruder struck a wheel-horse square in the barrel, passing clear through him and between the driver's legs. The horse pitched forward on his nose while the rider rolled over in the mud, turning upon his hands and feet, face upwards, with a look of "who-got-the-worst-of-it" on his countenance, but did not utter one word. I think that driver was none other than the genial Gen. James S. Fraser of New York City.

I had been back to order up the horses to comply with General Kearney's orders to move a section to the front, etc., and while returning met Gen. Joe. Dickinson, Hooker's Assistant Adjutant-General, now an official of the Pension Bureau in Washington, a few rods in the rear of the guns. A large mud hole caused each to turn to the right, leaving a space of about ten or twelve feet between us as we passed. At this moment a six-pound ball struck in the mud between us, splashing the dirty water over each and ricocheting, bounded away to the rear. A glance and a shake of the head was all the comment made as we parted, neither realizing at the time the value of that mud hole.

The advance up the Peninsula was one continued

struggle to extricate the carriages from the sticky mud. Our Division did not meet the enemy again until after crossing the Chickahominy River; then began a series of contests, ending with the Seven Days' battles. The fatigue and exposure to the elements were very trying.

June 30th the Battery took part in the Malvern Hills battle. (I must rely upon information obtained from those who were present, being absent myself from June 12th to July 5th on sick leave.)

On my rejoining the Battery at Harrison's Landing, Va., General Hunt, Chief of Artillery Army of the Potomac, stated to me verbally that two or three officers of the U. S. Army had reported to him that during the engagement of June 30th the Battery had killed an officer and two privates of the Union troops by firing into our own line, and he desired me to investigate the matter, which I did.

I was further informed by the General that it was reported that canister was used at a distance of eighteen hundred yards. I knew that there was not a man in the company who would be guilty of such an exhibition of ignorance regarding range and ammunition, but an investigation was necessary, which I made, with the following result:

First, I learned that not one round of canister had been used since the battle of Williamsburg. This was very easy to figure out. The complement, it is well known, is fifty rounds of canister to each gun, and as that amount was on hand, while none had been drawn on requisition, it was evidently an error as to that part of the report.

As to the killing of our own men, every man in the

company emphatically denied even the possibility of such a catastrophe, explaining to me the position of the enemy and the direction of the Battery's fire. I was firmly convinced at the time that a mistake had been made as to the name of the battery responsible for such gross mismanagement, and was led to believe that General Hunt shared my opinion, after learning the particulars as above related, and I had reason to believe at the time that the reputation of the Battery had not suffered by the unfortunate error, but that all had been satisfactorily explained. Twenty-eight years after the occurrence alluded to above, I read with much regret and surprise the following report, dated Harrison's Landing, July 5th, 1862:

* * * "The fight was too unequal and was apparently so considered by the New York Battery on my right. The conduct of this Battery I have already reported verbally to the General commanding the Division and also to the Adjutant-General of the Army of the Potomac. I here renew that report in writing. It called itself the 4th New York, and was commanded by a Lieutenant Nairn. I believe there is the amplest evidence that it killed an officer and two enlisted men of our own. However that may be, I can assert from my own knowledge that if terrible at all it was only so to its friends. It fired quite rapidly, making considerable noise and smoke, but it fired canister at a distance of from fifteen to eighteen hundred yards. Round after round of canister was fired, and so far as I could observe nothing else was until long after friend and foe had ceased firing. This irrepressible Battery threw several case shot or shell which struck somewhere, certainly much nearer our own troops than the point at which the hostile battery had been posted. * * *

"(Signed)   STEPHEN H. WEED,
"*Captain 5th U. S. Artillery.*"

From the date of the foregoing report it is evident that my investigation was made subsequent to it, and yet not one word in regard to it is found on record in the published reports. The testimony is *ex-parte*, inasmuch as the explanation has been excluded, hence the charge stands boldly recorded in history, while the defence made at that time has been denied a hearing.

I am convinced that these gentlemen of the regular army would have modified their opinion had they understood the facts as herein stated. No doubt they were honest in their convictions, but by comparing notes and explaining the position held by the Battery at the time the alleged "wild firing" occurred, I am certain it could have been clearly shown that the Battery was mistaken for some other.

At this late day it is useless to attempt a defense beyond an impartial statement of facts. General Weed was killed on Little Round Top July 2, 1863, an officer of unquestioned merit and integrity, whose motive in this unfortunate affair was evidently intended for the good of the service. Of the other two officers no doubt the same can be said. General Hunt, who appeared to never forget any incident of the slightest importance, has ceased to live. I therefore state what few facts still exist as a reasonable excuse for reopening a case which has been so long a matter of undisputed record, but carefully locked up with all other official papers in the War Department until Congress authorized their publication. Our defense is in the shape of an explanation, the only course left to us.

While located near Harrison's Landing, the Battery was placed on the outer line in a crude fortification within the Third Corps lines. While so posted President Lincoln visited the Army of the Potomac and examined the breastworks, coming towards our position without the slightest warning being given to us—during his tour of inspection—and when within a distance of less than twenty-five yards, Captain McKeever rode up and directed that a salute be fired, so the President was compelled to halt until the firing ceased, when he passed between the guns and limbers, while the men loudly cheered him.

CHAPTER VI

Fredericksburg.

AUGUST 15th began the march on the retreat towards Yorktown, Va., where we arrived in due time, and after a delay of some days we succeeded in getting transportation for the carriages to Alexandria, Va.; the horses were shipped two or three days later. We did not reach Alexandria in time to participate in Pope's campaign, at the front, but rendered service in and around the defenses.

The Second Battle of Bull Run, like the First, was disastrous to the Union Army, and impartial history has verified the bitter accusations of the rank and file at the time, that their defeat was due to the incapacity of those to whom was entrusted the management and maneuvering of that splendid body of men known as The Army of the Potomac. These swarthy veterans of the innumerable fights, skirmishes and marches of the Peninsula deserved a better fate than met them at Manassas.

None that died in this ill-starred campaign was more generally mourned than gallant, dashing Phil. Kearny, the Murat of our Army, the idol of the soldiers who served under him.

Killed just at dusk on the field of Chantilly, his body was sent into our lines under Confederate escort with instructions to be delivered to General Hooker. As the ambulance which contained all that was mortal of the bravest man that ever drew a sword passed Fort Ward with its blind-folded escort in gray, many an old soldier, hardened to death and wounds in every shape, shed tears, and when General Hooker received the remains of his gallant friend whom he should never look upon again with the exultant light of battle in his dauntless eyes, he could only say between his sobs, "such is the curse of war."

There was another soldier laid low at Manassas, though not to die, fit to be named on the same page with brave Phil. Kearny. He wore neither stars nor bars, the modest chevrons of a corporal denoting but one remove from the rank of private. He was then unknown outside of his own company, and when an exploding shell crushed his legs into a shapeless mass of flesh and bones it was only one enlisted man less in the regiment, one of the numerous "killed, wounded and missing" reported by the papers in round numbers. But when this maimed youth's vigorous tenacity and ambition enabled him to survive the surgeon's knife, to make his way through the crowded walks of life to that place in the front ranks accorded only to acknowledged force and ability, then the world came to know that the mangled boy carried off the bloody field of Bull Run was one whom his country delights to honor, and who is proud to bear the title he bore then—CORPORAL TANNER.

Hooker's Division, then commanded by General D. E. Sickles, and to which the Battery was still attached, was selected to remain near Washington during the Antietam campaign. I was designated as Chief of Division Artillery by virtue of the date of my commission. My duties were subsequently enlarged by General Barry, who directed that the field batteries located between, and at, Arlington and Alexandria, Va., should be subject to my control for inspection, etc. I relinquished the executive control of the Battery to Lieut. J. E. Nairn, but remained with it for the time being.

On a certain date about midnight, General Sickles received information of an intended raid by Stuart's cavalry on Falls Church, Va., where two small forts had been erected, and where the 120th New York Volunteers, Col. G. H. Sharpe, which had just entered the service, were stationed.

I was directed to send a battery at once. I took my own to save time, and went myself, because I was personally familiar with the locality. This knowledge was essential on account of the extreme darkness of the night. We reached Fort Buffalo between 2 and 3 o'clock A. M., and the guns were soon in position; then Colonel Sharpe desired me to visit the outposts with him, which I did.

The infantry had been well placed and everything put in shape to make the reception warm in case of an attack. The Colonel was very active and did not propose to give me an opportunity for sleep, as he compelled me by his presence to remain on the *qui vive*.

The enemy did not put in an appearance, however, to our great relief.

The Division was reviewed by President Lincoln and the members of his Cabinet, while occupying the defenses of Washington. Again the Battery had the honor of firing the salute for the President.

On this occasion I commanded at least ten batteries, passing before the President in review, battery front. They made a splendid appearance. The President instructed me to say to the battery commanders that he was very much gratified with the fine, soldierly appearance of the artillery, shaking me by the hand warmly while speaking.

At General Sickles's suggestion the artillery was notified in special orders as to the President's complimentary and flattering comments.

Soon after this, November 4th, the Division moved out to Manassas Junction, acting as a provisional command, charged with the responsibility of putting and keeping in order the railroad, opening as it were, a line of communication by which the Army of the Potomac could be furnished with supplies at a point where its line of march intercepted that of the railroad. The Battery was pushed out as far as Catlett Station, where the bridge had been destroyed, it having been partly burned by the enemy. This route was kept open until after the Army had passed on its way to Falmouth, Va.

In the winter of '62 Gen. Geo. B. McClellan, after being relieved of command, returned to Washington at this time on one of the trains over this road.

Having performed the duty assigned it, the Division took up the line of march to Falmouth, Va. At Wolf Run Shoals General Patterson shot himself, and the Battery was detailed to fire a blank at intervals of thirty minutes between sunrise and sunset, as a token of respect to his memory and rank. Arriving at Falmouth, we rejoined the Corps, from which we had been separated since before the battle of Antietam.

Preceding the battle of Fredricksburg the following order was received:

"HEADQUARTERS ARMY OF THE POTOMAC,
"*December* 8, 1862.

"Major-General HOOKER,
"*Commanding Center Grand Division.*

"*General:* The commanding General directs that you will please have issued to each of the following named battery commanders the accompanying order, and take the necessary steps to have it executed: Lieut. Hazlett, Battery "D," 5th U. S. Artillery, Griffin's Division; Captain Smith, 4th New York Battery, Sickles's Division.

"Very respectfully, your obedient servant,
"(Signed.) JOHN G. PARKER,
"*Chief of Staff.*

(Sub-inclosure.)

"*The Commanding Officer*,
"*Battery* ———.

"*Sir:* You will report in person to Lieut.-Colonel Hayes, commanding artillery, at the office of Brigadier-General Hunt, Chief of Artillery, at 10 A. M., Wednesday, the 10th instant. You will obey, until you are ordered to rejoin your Division, such orders as you may receive from Lieut.-Colonel Hayes, or Brigadier-General Hunt, Chief of Staff."

Reporting as above ordered, my instructions were to lead certain batteries to a point designated, between dark and daylight, on a certain date; said batteries were then assigned to localities commanded by either Colonels Tompkins or Hayes. Having disposed of all the Division artillery, being Chief of the same, I requested permission to re-assume command of the 4th New York Battery, which was granted.

This Battery was posted on Falmouth Heights, directly opposite the Confederate works above and west of Fredericksburg, and south from our position about eighteen hundred or two thousand yards. It was expected that a pontoon bridge would be thrown over the river near this point, by which means troops could be placed in the town.

Early on the morning of December 12, 1862, about 3 o'clock A. M., I discovered, by seeing them march past street lamps, the flickering light of which betrayed their movements, that the enemy were moving troops in the edge of the town near the river bank. I concluded that they were placing sharpshooters in the cellars under the buildings on the bank of the river (to pick off our artillerists, I thought at the time).

General Hunt, who appeared to be in the saddle all the time, and constantly on the move, visited us several times during the night, and I related to him what I had seen. It is my impression that he informed me that by a mutual agreement between the Provost Marshals of the Army of the Potomac and that of Northern Virginia, troops would not occupy the town; be this as it may, when our engineers began to construct a bridge (known in history as the Upper Bridge) about

6 A. M., they were greeted with a few volleys fired by men hidden in the cellars on the opposite bank. It soon became evident that these Confederate marksmen would have to be routed before a bridge could be put down at this point.

After some delay it was arranged that the batteries, which were in position on the north bank, were to open and dislodge, if possible, the rebel infantry. Shortly after 8 A. M. a shower of shot and shell was poured into the different structures wherein the enemy lurked, then our firing ceased and the engineers tried to work; but the moment they did so, popping was resumed on the other side. This firing first from one side and then the other was continued at intervals until about 3 o'clock P. M., when volunteers were called for from the infantry to cross over in pontoon boats and drive the rebels from their holes.

Nearly one hundred men from the 7th Michigan promptly offered their services. While the boats were being loaded the firing increased, the bullets falling in the water near the boats like hail, but there was no flinching—the men who had willingly undertaken this task had counted the cost and fearlessly placed their lives on the altar of their country.

I thought, while gazing on this scene, that it would rank with any deed of daring recorded in the pages of history. Think of it! less than one hundred men exposed in three open, clumsy boats, propelled with oars or paddles, which made but slow progress, in the face of a well-concealed and active foe, having no knowledge of the numbers they were about to encounter, with little hope of reinforcements until the boats could return

—and all for thirteen dollars per month! No, there must have been something else—loyalty and true patriotism overcame all thought of self, and without the slightest ostentation they quietly went forward ready to meet any fate that might await them.

I shall never forget my sensations during the few moments required to cross the river. The first man to jump ashore from the boats was a lieutenant, who was hit before striking the ground. He crawled back into the boat and subsequently recrossed the river; as soon as a landing was made the men were hurried forward, when a running fight through the streets ensued; more men were rowed across, and finally the Rebel infantry were driven back and the engineers soon completed the bridge, over which a large force marched on the night of the 12th.

During the 11th and 12th a fitful cannonade was directed upon the town, with the intention of burning it down. The Battery was employed after the completion of the bridge in drawing the fire from the works opposite to relieve the troops while crossing. In this manner the assistance rendered was valuable and greatly aided the infantry, by covering them while reinforcing their comrades, who were on the other side.

The official report of this battle as to the participation of the Battery will furnish further particulars:

"CAMP NEAR FREDERICKSBURG, *December* 17, 1862.

"*Colonel:* I have the honor to submit the following report of the participation of the 4th New York Battery under my command, in the late bombardment of Fredericksburg. In obedience to orders from Headquarters Centre Grand Division, dated December 10,

1862, I reported to you, and was by you ordered to take command of the 4th New York Battery which had been under the executive command of 1st Lieut. J. E. Nairn since November 4th, I at that time assuming command of the Division Artillery, in compliance with orders from headquarters, Sickles's Division, of that date. Position was assigned me by you on the north bank of the river about five hundred yards west of the Lacey house, with instructions to obey all orders from General Hunt, Colonel Tompkins and yourself. I placed my guns in battery about 8:30 o'clock on the evening of the 11th, and set my men at work throwing up small breastworks around each gun as a protection against the enemy's sharpshooters. About 3 A. M. on the morning of the 12th, General Hunt ordered me to fire upon the town, when the battery adjoining my left ("K," 1st U. S. Artillery, Captain Graham), opened. In obedience to this order I opened fire about 5 A. M., (or soon after the enemy's sharpshooters opened fire upon the engineers who were constructing pontoon bridges). I kept up a rapid fire during the forenoon, damaging the vents of five guns, which became enlarged. On the 13th the enemy's batteries opened on the town and our men. I undertook to draw their fire by replying from my Battery, and several times during the day succeeded in checking the fire from some of their batteries on our right and in front of my position. During the 14th and 15th my orders were to fire upon the batteries in front whenever they opened upon our reinforcements or the town, which order I obeyed until ordered by General Hunt not to fire under any circumstances. Again during the night of the 15th I received orders from Colonel Tompkins to be on the alert to cover the retreat of our army; but as the enemy made no attempt to interfere I had no occasion to fire. The ammunition furnished me by Captain Young, ordnance officer of Sickles's Division, was of an inferior quality. The concussion projectiles (Parrott) were used as solid shot; the case shot worked poorly; about one in twelve exploded. The cartridges were composed of different kinds of powder or of various quantities, which made accuracy almost impossible. During the five days' firing I expended, all told, about sixteen hundred rounds of case shot and shell. I have no casualties to report. The non-commissioned officers and privates of the Battery conducted themselves admirably, obeying all orders with promptness. Lieutenants Nairn, Scott, McLean and Smith, by their attention to duty, contributed greatly to render the fire of the Battery effective. Lieutenant Nairn made several splendid shots, sighting the pieces himself. The officers have my warmest thanks.

"I am sir, very respectfully,
"Your obedient servant,
"(Signed.) JAMES E. SMITH."
"Lieutenant-Colonel WILLIAM HAYES,
"*Command Reserve Artillery.*"

The vents were so much enlarged that vent tenders were compelled to cover them with the hand instead of the thumb, and not being able to use a friction-primer by reason of this enlargement, the *papier maché* or slow match was substituted; by this means fire was continued until dark, when General Hunt sent from general headquarters of the army a competent mechanic, for whose convenience a tent was put up in rear, which covered the light necessary to complete this work, and into which one gun was run at a time until the entire six were revented with copper vents, which did not again fail us.

During the 11th the enemy's pickets were stationed across the river with stacked arms; no attempt was made to molest them and they disappeared during the night.

After four days and nights constantly exposed to the

inclemency of the weather, which was bitter cold, the ground covered with snow, no shelter or fire, defeat staring us in the face, every charge made by the infantry on the heights within our full view greatly adding to the mental strain already stretched to its fullest tension, we received the command to fall back, which, although not unexpected, was a great relief, and gladly we returned to camp to recuperate and prepare for the famous "mud march."

CHAPTER VII

After Fredericksburg. A Summer March through Maryland.

FATE appeared to be against General Burnside, at least the elements were, but the grand old army did n't mind it; defeat and disappointment could not discourage it. Therefore, when the order to march came again, promptly moved forward the same old Corps, the same old bronzed faces. I do not remember a single instance while the army was marching towards the enemy, where the *morale* was not most excellent; jokes were cracked and songs sung, which seemed more suited to a picnic excursion. An army composed of brain and muscle and minds capable of reasoning stood behind muskets; an army of intelligence and grit, it was certain of success in the end. The rank and file understood the principles involved and aimed to perform the work appertaining to their duties without regard to who might be in command. Do not understand me as saying that they had no preference in this respect; such was not the truth;

they simply disregarded their personal likes and dislikes and yielded loyal allegiance to all superiors. To conquer was the desire of all, and to this end their best energies were directed. The grandest army that ever trod the earth!—The Federal army of '61–'65.

Again the Battery left camp, January 20th, 1863, and for four days floundered and struggled in the mud while marching to the United States Ford and getting back to camp.

By direction of General Hunt I had control of twelve light batteries which were marched to a certain point, where I met and turned over to Colonel De Russey nine batteries. With the other three I was instructed to move to our right and reach the United States Ford. At twilight we entered a dense pine woods through which there was a narrow road leading to the river. Scarcely five hundred yards from the opening we encountered a pontoon train heading in the opposite direction and which was firmly mired in the mud; the colored drivers were either stupidly drunk or too wildly excited to know what they were doing. Everything was in confusion. My orders were to reach United States Ford; one Battery (my own, 4th New York) cut its way around the train and camped as near the Ford as prudence allowed. The other two did not make it.

The infantry were compelled to construct a corduroy road before the Battery could retreat. Finally, after five days (20th to 24th inclusive) hard work for men and horses, for the second time during this winter we returned to our old camping ground. During the balance of the winter the Battery was subjected to much harsh treatment and many disorganizing changes and incidental disagreements that seriously impaired its efficiency. In consequence of various transfers, resignations, etc., I became ranking artillery officer of the Third Corps, and, in accordance with the Army regulations, Chief of the Corps Artillery. This compelled me to relinquish control of and sever my connection with the Battery. This was followed by the resignation of Lieut. J. E. Nairn, and the command of the Battery devolved upon Lieut. C. H. Scott, an officer totally unfitted for the position. He was ordered before a Board of Examining Officers, and it resulted in his discharge by order of the Secretary of War. Lieut. Wm. T. McLean, the next officer in command, appeared before the same Board and passed a creditable examination. Lieut. E. S. Smith, who had been promoted, together with McLean, vice Nairn and Scott, was transferred to Battery "K," 4th U. S. Artillery, and a Lieutenant Goodman, 6th New Jersey Infantry (with whom Lieutenant Smith traded off) transferred from Battery "K" to the 4th New York.

Before this took place, General Birney, commanding 1st Division, made application for another battery—having but three while the 2d Division had five. I was directed to send one battery from the 2d Division to report to him. The order was issued to General Berry, commanding 2d Division, who referred the matter to Captain Osborne, Chief of Division Artillery, and he designated the 4th New York as the Battery to be transferred. This created a very ill feeling on the part of the men. Except Battery "H," 1st U. S. Artillery, the Battery had been attached to the Division longer than any other serving with it, and the men believed they were being discriminated against and refused to move from the park when ordered.

This being reported to Headquarters Third Corps, General Berry was notified, who declared that the Battery no longer belonged to his command. Then General Birney was notified, and he detailed the 40th New York Volunteers with instructions to move or bury the Battery.

Under these circumstances a transfer was made without further trouble, but much of the interest and pride usually felt by those who had shared hardships and dangers together was, to a certain extent, diminished and their ardor dampened. The men were despondent and became lax in their duties, not without some excuse. Finally, a Lieutenant Barstow of the U. S. Artillery was assigned to the command, when matters went from bad to worse, culminating in unwise and ill-advised promotions.

If I had remained blind to all that concerned my old Battery, my personal interests would have been benefited, my position as chief of Corps Artillery, with ten batteries to control, and a good prospect for the creation of a brigade with the usual staff, making it one of the most desirable commands in the army. I had already submitted a proposition to General Hooker, then commanding the Army of the Potomac, with a view to organizing the Corps artillery as above stated, and was instructed to again submit my proposition after the then-pending movement (Chancellorsville).

This was afterwards carried out by Captain Randolph, my successor, and the artillery so brigaded.

My position was all I could desire, but should have

had a higher rank to correspond with my command. As a Captain I controlled ten field batteries, while the date of my commission deprived me of the privilege of assuming command of my own Battery, under army regulations.

After the assignment of a United States officer to the command of the Battery, and the consequent demoralization, I determined to resign my commission and get reappointed, by which proceeding the question of date of rank would be settled, and I could return to my original command. Therefore, on the 26th day of April, 1863, I tendered my resignation and received an honorable discharge. Having provided myself with proper letters to present to the Governor of the State of New York, I returned from the army to Washington, D. C., and on May 4th presented my letters in person to Governor Seymour at Albany, N. Y., who accorded me an audience.

After explaining my reasons for resigning and again applying for a re-appointment to the same position, I was soon in possession of a new commission bearing date of issue.

When I returned to Washington, D. C., Chancellorsville battle had been fought, and the Army of the Potomac had returned for the third time to its camps near Falmouth, Va. The Battery marched during this series of battles with the First Division, and held several positions of importance, but was not called on to open fire.

Early in June I reported for muster at Headquarters Third Corps, but General Sickles being absent, sick, it was decided to defer it until his return.

The Corps broke up camp on the 11th, and began

the campaign of Gettysburg. I offered my services as volunteer aid to General Birney, commanding the Corps, and so acted until we reached Brandy Station, Va., where I took the cars for Washington, D. C.

I soon found General Sickles, who directed me to be on the lookout, as he intended to start for the front when he could reach the army by rail, and that by so doing I could go with him. On June 27th he started by special train on the B. & O., from Relay House. We made slow progress owing to a report that "Guerrillas" were raiding the country through which we were passing, but beyond this we had no trouble, and reached Frederick, Md., about 1 o'clock next morning.

Besides General Sickles and aids, there were on this train General Marston and Colonel Hardie, the latter bearer of despatches relieving General Hooker of the command of the Army of the Potomac. (We were not informed of the nature of his business, however.)

We found the Corps halted east of Frederick City where we rejoined it, and my muster was made without delay, and again I was at the head of the Battery. A hasty inspection put me in possession of its condition, which was more favorable than I had dared to hope.

The march from here through upper Maryland was the most delightful we had made during our service. It was harvest time; the weather was superb, and the roads fairly good through a beautiful country which had tasted but little of the destructive havoc of war. The old familiar sights of great fields of yellow wheat, orchards loaded with fruit, wide, green stretches of pasture and meadow-land, snug farm-houses and huge red-roofed barns, made it seem a pleasure trip after the hardships of the campaign in Virginia. Then the boys very soon discovered that there was a very fair supply of most excellent apple-jack along the route, as this was considered by the farmers a prime necessity in the arduous labors of harvest. It is true it was a little difficult to get at, as these rural citizens had doubtless heard of the partiality ever shown by soldiers towards this famous Southern commodity. It was usually hidden in various out-of-the-way places about the farms, and it required much ingenious diplomacy to ascertain the whereabouts of the concealed treasure. When all else failed, a party of thirsty soldiers would frequently march into a barn-yard, attach a couple of fine horses and coolly inform the alarmed farmer that they were required for the Government service. Upon his remonstrating, the leader of the gang would take him to one side and suggest that, as he appeared to be a decent kind of a fellow they would n't be hard on him, and if he had anything like apple-jack, or peach-brandy, or even plain whiskey about the place, they would compromise the matter. They always got it.

Another source of constant enjoyment was the Third Corps Band, which appeared to be ubiquitous. They were always in the lead on the march, and yet when passing through the numerous villages on our route we would find them located on some balcony or front porch or grouped around the town pump discoursing lively martial airs as we gayly passed by with banners flying and singing loyal songs, while ladies and children would, sometimes, be waving handkerchiefs from their door yards.

It was, indeed, a gay and jolly march, such as seldom fell to our lot, but to many brave boys it was a march to death, for its end was the bloodiest field of the war—Gettysburg, and but two days away.

We reached Emmittsburg, Md., in the afternoon of July 1st., and after a short halt the Corps moved forward towards the Pennsylvania line, while my Battery and Winslow's were left here with Burling's and De Trobriand's Brigades to guard the Hagerstown road.

Gen. Burling's official report refers to this detail as follows:

* * * "I was ordered by Maj. Hamlin, Assistant Adjutant-General, Second Division, Third Army Corps, to remain at this place .with the Brigade and Smith's Battery to guard the Hagerstown road. In conjunction with Colonel Sewell, of the 5th New Jersey Volunteers, and Captain Smith of the Battery, I immediately made such disposition of my command as I deemed advisable to accomplish this object. * * *

"(Signed)   BURLING,
"*Commanding Brigade.*"

About 1.30 on the morning of the fateful 2d of July, orders were received from Gen. Meade to re-join the Corps at Gettysburg, eleven miles away.

It required some time to withdraw the pickets, therefore it was 4 A. M. before we were ready to move forward, rejoining the Corps and Division at 9 o'clock A. M.

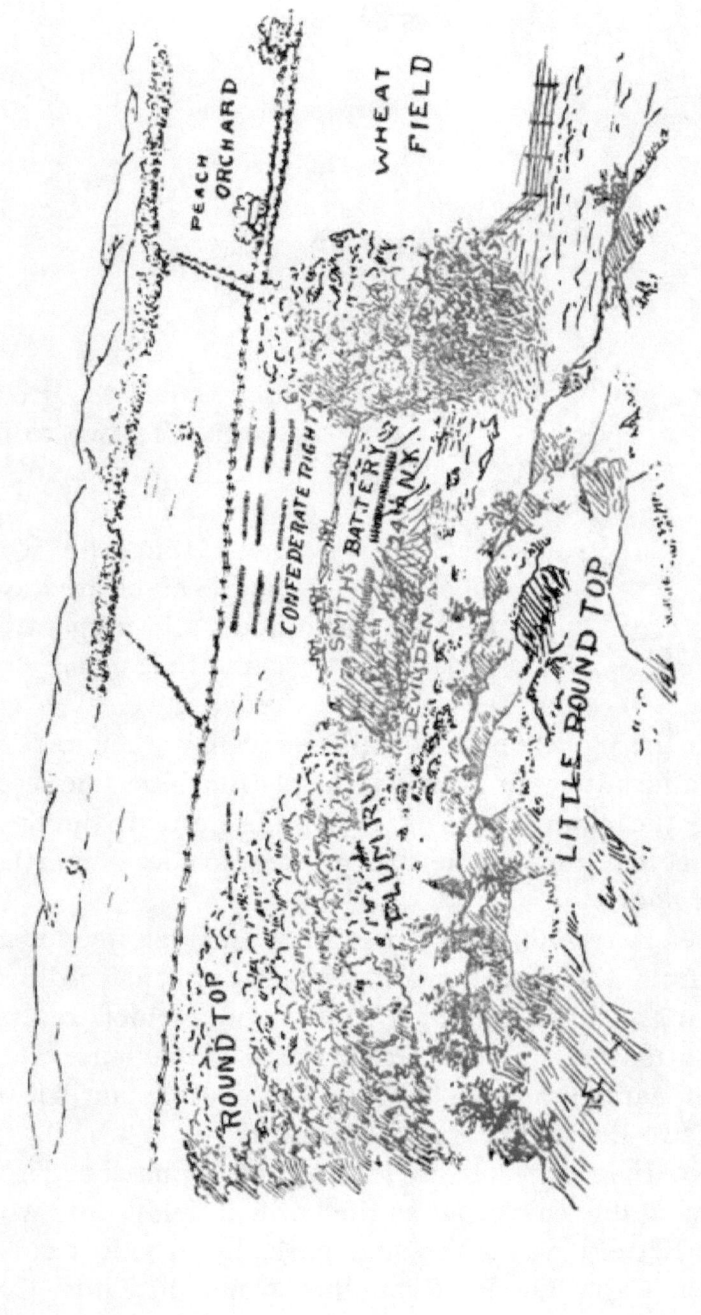

CHAPTER VIII

Gettysburg.

AS we approached the ground between the two armies in the vicinity of the "peach orchard," I noticed that the fences had been cleared away and all preparations made that usually preceded a battle; even then the pickets and skirmishers were uneasy and kept up a desultory fire, little puffs of thin blue smoke dotting the plain before us, indicating quite distinctly the respective lines of the two greatest armies on earth, at this hour.

Before reaching the "orchard" an aide came towards us from the direction of the "wheat-field" riding at great speed and waving a white handkerchief to attract our attention. A halt was made in consequence and we then learned that our position was equi-distant between the two lines and somewhat critical.

No time was lost in leaving the Emmitsburg road, moving due east as far as the "wheat-field," into which the Battery was taken and parked. About 1 o'clock P. M. Capt. G. E. Randolph, Chief of Third Corps

Artillery, piloted the Battery to "Devil's Den," pointing to a steep and rocky ridge running north and south, indicating that my guns were to find location thereon.

From the termination of the ridge at the "Den" to the woods dividing the "wheatfield" from the valley of Plum Run, the distance was not more than fifty yards. Here I could not place more than four guns on the crest. In rear of this ridge the ground descended sharply to the east, leaving no room for the limbers on the crest, therefore they were posted as near to the guns as the nature of the declivity permitted. The remaining two guns were stationed in rear about seventy-five yards, where they could be used to advantage, covering the Plum Run Gorge passage, which lies to the south of and below the crest.

The four guns could not be depressed to reach troops moving through the gorge, hence the necessity for this arrangement.

Two regiments of infantry, viz: the 4th Maine, Colonel Walker, and the 124th New York, Colonel Ellis, were formed so as to cover the open space between the woods and base of Round Top; the former being on the extreme left, while the latter, the "Orange Blossoms," were directly in rear of the four guns.

I felt anxious about our left flank and made an effort to get some infantry posted in the woods along the base of Round Top, but as the enemy gave little time for reflection, my attention was occupied in looking after the Battery, and replying to the concentrated fire of a number of guns.

This artillery battle began about 2 P. M., and was a trial of skill between artillerists. The accuracy of the enemy's aim was astonishing, while that of the gunners of the Battery may be judged from the reports of those who have the best right to know. (See Confederate reports.)

About 3.30 o'clock the enemy's infantry appeared in line of battle, moving directly upon the Round Tops. The four guns were now used to oppose and cripple this attack and check it as far as possible. I never saw the men do better work ; every shot told ; the pieces were discharged as rapidly as they could be with regard to effectiveness, while the conduct of the men was superb ; but when the enemy approached to within three hundred yards of our position the many obstacles in our front afforded him excellent protection for his sharpshooters, who soon had our guns under control. At the fence at the base of the slope, which gently declines to the west in front, they make a short halt, then press on ; we use canister without sponging, but are firing at a disadvantage for the reason just stated, to save the guns. Colonel Ellis and Colonel Walker now advance their commands, and, dashing through the Battery, charge upon the Confederates with great impetuosity. My fire is withheld until the front is uncovered by the falling back of the "Orange Blossoms" and 4th Maine ; again the artillerists spring to their guns ; the 99th Pennsylvania Volunteers move along a point in rear of the guns, and boldly take position above the Den.

The 4th Maine on the left, with a line across the mouth of the gorge, have been forced back; the situation is most critical; I ask for assistance. General Hunt has told me how important it is to hold this position to the last. The enemy are pressing on the left, while those in front and to the right-front are advancing skirmishers. My guns are again in danger of capture. The brave "Orange Blossoms" have been withdrawn; the 4th Maine and 99th Pennsylvania have retired. In reply to my earnest plea for help I have been asked to hold on for thirty minutes, when succor would surely come; if the guns are to be saved it must be done now at the risk of exposing our weakness. What is best to do under the circumstances becomes a momentous question.

I finally determine to consume the time it will take to remove the guns in fighting them, and thus trade them for time, if it becomes necessary. The men are instructed to remove all implements if they are compelled to fall back, so that our pieces may not be turned against us. The bold front presented by the Battery cause the enemy to approach it gingerly; but alas! we are flanked by the enemy moving through the gorge by the right flank; our four pieces are now useless, but the two in rear can be of service. I run with all the speed in me and open fire with these two guns on the troops coming through the gorge.

The enemy are taken by surprise; their battle flag drops three different times from the effect of our canister. Thrice their line wavers and seeks shelter in the woods, but in a moment they return in a solid mass. The 6th New Jersey moves forward from the "wheatfield" across my front, cutting off the fire of the two pieces; then the 40th New York passes through the park of the horses and carriages stationed near the position occupied by the two guns, and attacks Benning's Brigade.

I now conclude to save the balance of the Battery, if possible, and have the fence lowered that it may pass through to the "wheat-field," but still hold it ready to make a further sacrifice, if deemed necessary. The four guns remain suspended, as it were, on the crest between the lines. I appeal to Colonel Egan to save them; he promises, but fails to fulfill his promise; the odds are too great against us.

The men have faced every danger; two brave men can do more than one—the one is on our side, the two are opposed to us. Finally the Federal infantry fall back. I have sent the carriages into the woods, and closely watch the enemy's movements.

At this time the report of Hazlett's guns from the summit of Little Round Top announces the arrival of assistance, none too soon, for Benning's Brigade, after pushing through the gorge, is about to cross the "Valley of Death" to take possession of the goal for which he has been fighting for more than two hours. The race is a sharp one; the Federals win it. The two guns are run through the woods, and seeing Winslow's Battery in position, I take position on his right just as he limbers up and retires.

Looking for the cause I perceive the enemy swarming from the woods and I lose no time in falling back.

Before the crest was abandoned, one of the four guns, having been disabled, was withdrawn; this left but three and these were taken off by the enemy after dark.

I mistook the "Orange Blossoms" for the 4th Maine, who were in our immediate rear when the artillery duel opened, and in my official report make no mention of this gallant regiment whose daring charge rendered such valuable and timely assistance.

At no time during the day had we more than two regiments of foot at one time engaged in defending this important point. The Battery was on the ground from 2 until 6 o'clock P.M.

By a careful comparison of the official reports herewith, it is shown that the impression of many of the Confederates is erroneous as to Little Round Top's occupation by Federals, and that they suffered from the fire of guns on its summit while advancing to the assault of Devil's Den. If this was true, then those who were on the line at the Den must have known it, as the fire from Little Round Top would have to pass over their heads.

In conclusion, let me say in further explanation of the loss of my guns, that three times during the day I could have withdrawn them without giving grounds for censure. It has usually been considered proper to retire a field battery when its infantry support falls back. Had this course been adopted the guns might have been saved, but the delay imposed upon the enemy was of inestimable value to the Federal army and more than offset the loss of the pieces. For instance, forty minutes elapsed between the departure of the infantry from the ridge and the arrival of the two regiments at the position in rear of it. Every one of those minutes contained sixty seconds and into each second was crowded a lifetime.

It had not occurred to me to save the Battery; indeed, I could not see how I was to do it without abandoning the defense of the valley and Little Round Top, but the arrival of the 6th New Jersey and the 40th New York Volunteers changed the situation somewhat. I felt that the responsibility was, at least, divided.

During the interval which occurred between the time we left the ridge and the coming of the two regiments, it appeared to me that the defense of the key to the Federal position depended upon the efforts of the men who were handling the two guns, and I now believe, laboring as I doubtless was, under the excitement and strain brought about by the severe ordeal and, may I say, peculiar features of the conflict, that my mental faculties were not in condition to take under consideration the probabilities and advisability of withdrawing from the contest while a gun could be discharged.

After the abandonment of the crest I felt personally responsible for the defense of the position, until Colonel Egan and Lieutenant-Colonel Gilkison with their regiments, entered the valley. (I do not intend to reflect upon General Ward and the balance of his brigade, but they were engaged more to the right and in the woods —hence the idea that further assistance from this quarter was impossible). This seemed to give me time for thought, and when the report of Hazlett's guns from Little Round Top proclaimed in thunder tones that our friends were near, every sound in the air appeared to ring with the welcome tidings that the victory was ours: that a new lease of life, so to speak, was granted to us. Under such a state of affairs may I not be pardoned for retiring the men who had so nobly remained at their posts and who had not taken advantage of the many opportunities they had had to fall back during the day, without incurring the least blame for so doing. The wounded who had not been sent to the field-hospital were placed upon the caissons and limbers, and every care taken to avoid confusion. The Battery was retired at a slow walk with the guns in rear.

I do not wish to be understood as reflecting on the infantry. Braver men never stood shoulder to shoulder with their faces to the foe. The peculiar features of this conflict and the nature of the ground made it possible, nay, quite possible, for the enemy to suppose that the woods and many large boulders concealed a hidden foe; hence, it was not strange that the Battery was permitted to stand as long as it did, but while our infantry were in sight they drew the fire of a force far superior as to numbers; besides they were more exposed than the few men who managed the pieces.

After the ridge was under control of the Confederate infantry, the Federal infantry, which had formed the defense to this part of the line, instead of retiring in the direction of Little Round Top, naturally fell back into the woods occupied by the balance of Ward's Brigade.

Lieutenant-Colonel Gilkison moved his regiment through the woods from the "wheat-field" in rear of the brigade and without seeing it. I venture to say that, inasmuch as Lieutenant-Colonel Gilkison has not been mentioned in any of the general reports for the gallant and timely aid rendered, the presence of his regiment was unknown to the brigade commander. Colonel Egan was guided by Captain Bristow of General Birney's staff. The troops that were stationed on the first line were relieved, after the charge had been repulsed and their ammunition expended, while those two regiments that came last upon the scene were not; they fell back before the advance of Benning's Brigade.

No blame can attach to any troops that fought in the Valley of Plum Run July 2d; the fault lay in their weakness, nothing else.

Colonel Walker misunderstood me, if I am to judge by the tone of his letter published in 1886. I certainly never said that I did not want his help; I was not fool enough to think a Battery could maintain a position such as was assigned to the 4th New York without a strong force of infantry in support. Not having such support in line, it was my belief that the best disposition ought to be made of the limited force at hand; therefore I suggested to Colonel Walker the advisability of moving his regiment from the rear of the Battery into the woods on our left, saying at the time, if he would protect the flank, the Battery would endeavor to take care of the front.

I believed at the time that infantry stationed in those woods would be able to resist any effort of the enemy to take possession of, and turn to good account, the excellent protection there offered. My desire to have Federal troops posted in the woods on our left and in front of Round Top, led to my speaking to Colonel Walker about the matter.

I regret that this brave old hero now attempts to place me in a false position; there was no mistaking my meaning at the time, and there is no good reason for misconstruing it now.

A few minutes before leaving the last position my horse was killed, which led to a ludicrous incident at my expense. I wore boots with a stiff leg to the knee and a light calf leg lined with white morocco reaching to the hip. When dismounted the upper part was rolled in a manner to form a top-boot; becoming disarranged during the battle the roll relapsed so that from the knee to the ankle the appearance was that of boots with white legs. Lieutenant Goodman seeing that I was without a mount, kindly gave me the use of his horse so that I might reach the head of the column then moving through the woods. While moving back from the position taken on Winslow's right, one of the men caught me by the leg exclaiming, "Captain, you're shot!" Glancing down I saw that the boot was covered with blood, and located the supposed wound in the calf of the right leg. The limb began to pain and I plainly felt the blood running into the boot. I moved my toes and the red liquid swashed between them. The foot and the limb were much swollen I imagined, and I became anxious to ascertain the extent of the damage; therefore, at the first available moment I was down. Calling one of the men to assist in drawing off the boot (scolding him for causing, unnecessarily, extra pain by his carelessness, while doing so) I patiently and calmly resigned myself to the inevitable. The boot being removed and no sign of blood found, I quickly glanced at the man who had drawn it and saw on his face a broad grin. I hastily said, "Let me tell this story first, please."

Searching for an explanation, it was discovered that the horse was shot in the flank, and by spurring, the boot-leg had come in contact with the blood which flowed from the wound. Imagination accomplished the rest.

Another incident occurred which, under the circumstances, was amusing, and goes far towards displaying the comic side of the Irish character. At a time when the rebel riflemen were annoying the artillerists from their concealed shelter behind the large boulders, etc., Michael Broderick, detailed from the 11th Massachusetts Volunteers, and placed as driver on the Battery wagon, left his team which was out of danger and came forward to the crest where things were a little lively, and picking up a musket which had been dropped by one of the infantry, he was soon engaged with a foe who was evidently behind one of the boulders in front. Mike was oblivious to the bullets flying carelessly about; he simply had an eye on his man, and to even up chances, he too sought the friendly protection of a large rock. His strange antics first attracted my notice, and when I took him to task for leaving his team, his reply was: "Let me stay here, Captain, sure there are plenty back there to look after the horses." I said no more and Mike again commenced to dance, first on one side of the rock and then on the other, challenging *his man* to come out and face him; then he would dodge behind the rock to avoid, I presume, the privilege of stopping a bullet, then out he would jump again shouting, "Come on now, if you dare, bad luck to you." He was thus engaged when I last noticed him. At night Mike was reported missing, but early on the morning of the 3d, he reported, with a rebel musket and cartridge belt, stating that he had been taken prisoner and placed in a belt of timber with other Federal soldiers. Watching his chance, he noticed the guards were few and far between, and when opportunity offered he quickly found a belt and musket and commenced to march up and down like the Confederate guards (his slouch hat and old blouse together with his general make-up aroused no suspicion, as many rebels were dressed similarly). When night came on he marched into the Federal lines and reported as stated.

The Battery was parked on the Baltimore pike. I sent to the Sixth Corps for a surgeon to care for the wounded. Early on the morning of the 3d I reported three guns for service and was assigned position in the second line near the Third Corps, but was not again engaged during this battle.

CHAPTER IX

Official Reports—Union

THE OFFICIAL REPORTS OF FEDERAL OFFICERS, FROM SERIES I, VOL. XXVII, PART I, REBELLION RECORDS.

GEN. H. J. HUNT, Chief of Artillery Army of the Potomac, relating to the part taken by the Battery at Gettysburg:

* * * "Smith's 4th New York on the extreme left and on a steep and rocky eminence in advance of Sugar Loaf, and on his right Winslow's ('D,' 1st New York) in a wheat-field, separated from Smith by a belt of woods. * * * As Smith had not opened, I went to his battery to ascertain the cause. When I arrived he had succeeded in getting his guns into position, and just opened fire. As his position commanded that of the enemy and enfiladed their line, his fire was very effective. * * * In the meantime the enemy had established his new batteries to the north of the road and Smith turned his guns upon them. * * * Three of these belonged to Smith's Battery on our extreme left. The guns were stationed on the brow of a very precipitous and rocky height, beyond a ravine in front of our line. The difficulty in getting these guns up the height had caused the delay in Smith's opening his fire. He fought them to the last moment in hopes of keeping the enemy off and in the belief that the ground would be in our possession again before the guns could be carried off by the enemy. He got off one of the four guns he had placed on the height, but was compelled to abandon the other three." * * *

Report of Major General David B. Birney, First Division, Third Corps:

* * * "Smith's battery of rifled guns was placed so as to command the gorge at the base of the Sugar Loaf Mountain." * * *

Report of Capt. George E. Randolph, Chief of Third Corps Artillery:

* * * "Smith's and Winslow's Batteries on their arrival from Emmitsburg were parked until some better disposition could be made of them. * * * I placed Smith's Battery near the extreme left, between Round Top Mountain and the woods, on a rocky hill commanding a long valley running toward Emmitsburg. On the right of Smith's, after passing a belt of woods, was an opening. * * * It soon became evident that the enemy was preparing for an attack at this point. He soon opened more batteries on the right of his first and commenced a heavy fire from them upon our troops. Ames and Clark were soon so well at work that the advantage was not on the side of the enemy, and at last a well-directed fire from Smith's Battery on the extreme left silenced them for a time. The respite, however, was short, as at about 3 o'clock P. M. the enemy re-opened fire, and, under cover of his artillery, began to push infantry against our position. The part of our line where Smith's Battery was placed was assailed in the most furious and determined manner, and notwithstanding the conduct of our troops, after a long struggle it became evident that the line would break. The hill upon which the guns stood was very rough and rocky, rendering maneuvering with horses almost an impossibility. Four of Captain Smith's guns only had been at first placed in battery. These were served

effectively till they could no longer be without danger to our own troops, who had advanced to the front of the battery. The remaining two were placed in a position a few yards in rear, and pointed obliquely into the woods on the left in front of Round Top Mountain, which was occupied by the advancing lines of the enemy. These guns continued their fire till their supports were compelled to retire, when they were withdrawn by Captain Smith, leaving three of the four that were in advance still on the hill and in possession of the enemy. Captain Smith says he supposed the hill would be immediately re-taken by our troops and that, as it was a place most difficult of access, it was wiser to leave them where they could be used against the enemy immediately we regained the hill. I regret the loss, but from my knowledge of the position and of the gallantry displayed by Captain Smith, I am convinced that it was one of those very unpleasant, but yet unavoidable, results that sometimes attend the efforts of the most meritorious officers." * * *

Report of Maj.-Gen. Sykes, U. S. Army, commanding Fifth Corps:

* * * "A rocky ridge, commanding almost an entire view of the plateau held by our army, was on our extreme left. Between it and the position occupied by Birney's Division, Third Corps, was a narrow gorge filled with immense boulders and flanked on either side by dense woods. It afforded excellent cover and an excellent approach for the enemy, both of which he promptly made use of. The rocky ridge commanded and controlled this gorge. In examining it and the ground adjacent previous to posting my troops, I found a battery at its outer edge and without adequate support. I galloped to General Birney, whose troops were nearest, explained to him the necessity of protecting the guns, and suggested that he should close his division on

the battery and hold the edge of the woods on its right. I promised to fill the gap he opened, which I did with Sweitzer's and Tilton's brigades, of my first division, posting them myself."

[NOTE.—I have been mystified by the above, and can not account for the scantiness of the support actually provided; it was not adequate, nor was it in harmony with the importance of the position.—J. E. S.]

Report of Thomas W. Egan, Colonel Commanding 40th New York Volunteer Infantry:

* * * "The enemy had at this time partly succeeded in flanking the Second Brigade upon my right by a movement upon their left. Captain Smith's (4th New York) Battery was stationed upon the ridge at my right and was in a very perilous situation; the enemy having already captured three of his pieces, he called upon me in beseeching terms to save his Battery." * * *

[NOTE.—It must be remembered that our front had changed when the 40th New York and 6th New Jersey regiments arrived. Our former front faced west, but after leaving the ridge we changed front to about southwest by south, to conform to the line made by Benning's Brigade, which had marched through the gorge by the right flank. (See map.) Therefore, when Colonel Egan speaks of his right he alludes to the ridge, and the troops on his right were the 6th New Jersey.—J. E. S.]

Report of Col. S. R. Gilkison, 6th New Jersey Infantry:

* * * "Advancing promptly through the woods we came to a fence. Having no one to guide me and not knowing the position the regiment was to occupy, I formed line and opened fire on the enemy directly in our front. Soon ascertaining the position of our line, under a heavy fire from the enemy, I advanced the regiment about two hundred yards across the open field directly in front of the 4th New York Battery, Captain Smith, taking position on the left of Ward's Brigade."

Report of Lieut. Charles F. Sawyer, 4th Maine:

* * * "Were then assigned position on the left of the Brigade and advanced to a position on a rocky hill, in support of the 4th New York Battery. The position of the regiment was changed to the left of the Battery on the advance of the enemy. One company ("F") being left on the brow of the hill, the rest of the regiment being in the ravine and left of the line extending into the side of the hill on the left." * * *

Report of Brig.-Gen. J. H. Hobart Ward, commanding Second Brigade and First Division:

* * * "After placing my Brigade in the position assigned, Major Stoughton, of the Second U. S. Sharpshooters, reported to me with his command. I directed him to advance his command as skirmishers across the field in front of mine for half a mile and await further orders. They had scarcely obtained the position designated before the skirmishers of the enemy issued from a wood in front, followed by heavy lines of infantry. Captain Smith's Battery of rifled guns posted on the eminence on my left, opened on the advancing enemy.
* * * In the meantime I had sent to General Birney for reinforcements, who directed Colonel Egan with the 40th New York, to report. The enemy now concentrated his force on our extreme left, with the intention to turn our left flank through a gorge between my left and Sugar Loaf Hill. The 40th New York was despatched to cover the gap, which they did most

effectually. Our men, now much exhausted and nearly destitute of ammunition, were relieved by a portion of the Second and Fifth Corps, when we retired and bivouacked for the night."

[NOTE—Benning's Brigade had made the passage of the gorge before the 40th New York volunteers reached the ground. The two pieces of Smith's Battery had been briskly engaged in pouring canister into the head column of these troops as they emerged from the gorge near Devil's Den. After this Benning formed his line between Little Round Top and Devil's Den, and then the 6th New Jersey and 40th New York Volunteers attacked them.—J. E. S.]

Report of Captain James E. Smith, 4th New York Battery:

"CAMP NEAR SANDY HOOK, MD., *July* 20, 1863.

"*Sir:* I have the honor to report the participation of the 4th New York Battery, under my command, during the Battle of Gettysburg July 2d. In compliance with instructions received from you, I placed two sections of my Battery on a hill near the Devil's Cave, on the left of General Birney's line, leaving one section together with caissons and horses, one hundred and fifty yards in the rear. The 4th Maine Regiment was detailed as support, forming line in rear, under cover of a hill. [This is an error; this position was occupied by the 124th New York Regiment.] On my left, extending half way to the Emmitsburg road, was a thick wood, in which I requested Lieutenant Leigh, aide-de-camp to General Ward, to place supports. He informed me that a brigade had already been placed there, but this must have been a mistake. About 2:30 P. M. the enemy opened fire on my right and front from several guns, directing a portion of their fire upon my position. I was ordered by one of General Ward's aides to return their fire, which order I complied with. Twenty minutes later I discovered the enemy was endeavoring to get a section of twelve-pounder guns in position on my left and front, in order to enfilade this part of our line; but I succeeded in driving them off before they had an opportunity to open fire. Soon after, a battery of six light twelve pounders marched from the woods near the Emmitsburg road and went in battery in the field in front about fourteen hundred yards distant. A spirited duel immediately began between this battery and my own, lasting nearly twenty minutes, when Anderson's Brigade of Hood's Division, Longstreet's Corps (rebel) charged upon us."

[NOTE.— This impression was formed at the time, based upon information obtained from some Confederate wounded soldiers left in their hospitals; it should have been Hood's Division.—J. E. S.]

"The rebel battery then left the field and I directed my fire upon the infantry. At this time I requested the officer in command of the 4th Maine Regiment to place his command in the woods on my left, telling him I could take care of my front, but my request was not complied with."

[NOTE.—It has been stated by some that I intimated my ability to whip the Confederate army with the Battery, and did not wish any support; but the truth of the matter is, I wished to place the support where it would do the most good. I felt very much annoyed that the woods to the left of our line, which offered such excellent protection for defensive operations, should be left for the enemy to enter without opposition. From this position the troops stationed on the ridge and across the ravine at Devil's Den were flanked, and under cover of these woods Benning formed his brigade for the march through the gorge, while the same woods furnished cover to Law's brigade to prepare for the assault on Round Top.—J. E. S.]

"I used case shot upon the advancing column until they emerged from the woods on my left flank in line of battle three hundred yards distant; then I used canister with little effect, owing to numerous large rocks which afforded excellent protection to their sharpshooters. I saw it would be impossible for me to hold my position without assistance, and therefore called upon my support, who gallantly advanced up the hill and engaged the enemy. Fighting became so close that I ordered my men to cease firing, as many of the 4th Maine had already advanced in front of the guns."

[NOTE.—This error as to the name of regiment was caused by my attention being directed to the front while the 4th Maine moved across the ravine, and the 124th New York occupied the vacancy in rear of the Battery. For many years I labored under the impression that the 4th Maine was directly in rear of the guns at the time I called for assistance. In this manner I failed to credit the "Orange Blossoms" with the noble and gallant charge they made at the most critical moment of that trying contest for the possession of the ridge and the guns stationed thereon.—J. E. S.]

"I then went to the rear and opened that section of guns, firing obliquely through the gulley (gorge), doing good execution. At this time the 6th New Jersey Volunteers, Lieutenant-Colonel Gilkison commanding, and 40th New York Regiment, Colonel Egan commanding came to our support. These regiments marched down the gulley fighting like tigers, exposed to a terrific fire of musketry; and when within one hundred yards of the rebel line the 4th Maine, which still held the hill, were forced to retreat."

[NOTE.—At the time the "Orange Blossoms" charged in front of the guns on the ridge cutting off my fire, I noticed the head of Benning's brigade moving by the flank through the gorge. To check this, I ran to the two guns in rear and opened with canister; seeing Federal soldiers on the ridge, I naturally supposed they were the same that had made the charge. Recent information leads me to believe the 99th Pennsylvania regiment was moved from the woods on the right, while the "Orange Blossoms" fell back into this same woods lower down the slope, after changing their front from west to south. It is certain that neither the 4th Maine nor "Orange Blossoms" occupied the ridge after my departure. In this way only can I account for the presence of the 99th Pennsylvania, which I failed to recognize at the time.—J. E. S.]

"Very soon afterward the 40th New York and 6th New Jersey regiments were compelled to follow. I then ordered my remaining guns to the rear. When I left these guns on the hill, one having been sent to the rear disabled, I was under the impression we would be able to hold that position; but, if forced to retreat, I expected my support would save the guns; which, however, they failed to do. I could have run my guns to the rear, but expecting to use them at any moment and the position being difficult of access, I thought best to leave them for a while. Again, I feared if I removed them the infantry might mistake the movement for a retreat. In my opinion, had supports been placed in the woods, as

I wished, the hill could not have been taken. I conducted my command to a field near the Baltimore turnpike — three-quarters of a mile from Third Corps headquarters — and encamped for the night, reporting three guns for service next morning to Captain Clark, acting Chief of Corps Artillery. * * * The non-commissioned officers and privates conducted themselves throughout the day with commendable bravery. * *
* I trust that no blame can be attached to me for the loss of any guns; I did that which in my judgment was best.

"(Signed)   JAMES E. SMITH."

CHAPTER X

Official Reports—Confederate

BEFORE calling attention to the official reports of Confederate officers engaged in our front and who make reference to the Battery, I wish to state that no other field pieces took part in the battle for the possession of the gorge and ridge near Devil's Den (Hazlett's not being in use until after the ridge had fallen into the enemy's possession, and the very nature of the positions forbids the admission of the theory advanced by some of the Confederates, that they suffered from the fire of guns stationed on Little Round Top while charging over the open space between the Devil's Den and Emmitsburg road); hence, all references here quoted apply to the 4th New York Battery, because I do not refer to that part of the battle for the possession of Little Round Top.

Report of Brig.-Gen. Henry L. Benning, Confederate States Army, commanding brigade:

* * * "A wood intervened between us and the enemy, which, though it did not prevent their shells from reaching us and producing some casualties, yet completely hid them from our view. On emerging from the woods their position became visible. Before us at the distance of six hundred or eight hundred yards, was an oblong mountain peak or spur, presenting to us a steep face much roughened by rocks. To the right four hundred or five hundred yards from the peak was the mountain itself, with a side that looked almost perpendicular; its summit overlooked the peak just sufficiently to command it well. On the summit of the peak were three pieces of artillery."

[NOTE.—This refers to the four guns, but as three were captured the mistake is obvious.—J. E. S.]

";On a sort of uneven, irregular shelf were three others. To the right and left of the Battery as well as immediately in its rear, were lines of infantry, as we afterwards ascertained. This formed the enemy's first line of battle."

[NOTE.—This description of the position of the Battery is accounted for by the manner in which this Brigade came through the gorge, as is the following statement in regard to Hazlett's guns. When General Benning first obtained a view of the second line it was after his brigade had reached the space between the gap and base of Little Round Top. At this time he had good reason to believe there was a second line, but he is a little premature in locating it.—J. E. S.]

"On the top of the mountain itself and a little to the right of the peak were five other guns. These commanded our approaches to the peak for nearly the whole way. To the right and left of these extended the enemy's second line of infantry. Where that line crossed the gorge running between the peak and the mountain, a point five or six hundred yards in the rear of the peak, were two other guns. This was ascertained when the right of the brigade reached the gorge by the terrible fire from them which swept down the gorge."

"Thus, what we had to encounter were thirteen guns and two, if not more, lines of infantry, posted on mountain heights. The intervening spur over which we had to march to reach the first line was nearly all open, * * * Where my line reached the foot of the peak (ridge) I found there a part of the 1st Texas, struggling to make the ascent, the rest of the brigade having gone to the right and left, the 4th and 5th Texas to the right and the 3d Arkansas to the left. The part of the 1st Texas referred to falling in with my brigade, the whole line commenced ascending the rugged steep and (on the right) crossing the gorge. The ground was difficult—rocks in many places—presenting by their precipitous sides insurmountable obstacles, while the fire of the enemy was very heavy and very deadly. The progress, therefore, was not very rapid, but it was regular and uninterrupted. After awhile the enemy were driven from their three front guns. The advance continued and at length they were driven completely from the peak, but they carried with them the three guns on its summit, its sudden descent on the other side favoring the operation, so that we captured only the three front guns. These were ten-pounder Parrotts. A number of prisoners were also taken, more, I suppose, than one hundred. * * * Colonel Jones was killed late in the action, not far from the captured guns, after the enemy's forces were driven from the position and they had themselves opened on it with shell from the other batteries, a fragment of one of which, glancing from the rock, passed through his brain. * * * Colonel Harris was farther to the right when he and his regiment were exposed to the terrible fire of the two pieces which swept the gorge, as well as to the infantry fire of the enemy's left. * * * Under a fire from so many cannon, and toward the last from so much musketry, they (the Confederates) advanced steadily over the ground, for the most part open, mounted a difficult height, drove back from it the enemy, occupied his lines, took three guns, captured a number of prisoners, and against his utmost efforts held all they had gained. The captured guns were taken by the 20th Georgia (Colonel Jones, and after his death, Lieutenant-Colonel Waddell), the part of the 1st Texas above referred to (Colonel Work), and the 17th Georgia (Colonel Hodges), but the honor of the capture was not exclusively theirs. They could not have taken, certainly could not have held, the guns, if Lieutenant-Colonel Harris, and, after his death, Major (W. S.) Shepherd, on the left with the 2d Georgia, and Colonel Du Boise, with the 15th Georgia, on the right, had not by the hardest kind of fighting and at great loss protected their flanks."

[NOTE.—The number of troops engaged in the capture of the guns, and the evidence of such brave foes, leaves little to be said as to the manner and character of the defense.—J. E. S.]

Report of Colonel William F. Perry, commanding 44th Alabama Infantry:

* * * "When at a short distance from the stone fence near the base of the mountain, General Law informed me that he expected my regiment to take a battery which had been playing on our line from the moment the advance began. This battery was situated not on the mountain itself, but on a rugged cliff which formed the abrupt termination of a ridge that proceeded from the mountain, and ran in a direction somewhat parallel with it, leaving a valley destitute of trees and filled with immense boulders between them. This valley, not more than three hundred paces in breadth, and the cliff on which their artillery was stationed, were occupied by two regiments of the enemy's infantry. The direction of the regiment after crossing the stone fence was such that a march to the front would have carried it to the right of the enemy's position. It was, therefore, wheeled to the left, so as to confront that position, its left opposite the battery and its right extending toward the base of the mountain. This movement was executed under fire, and within two hundred yards of the enemy. The forward movement was immediately ordered, and was responded to with an alacrity and courage seldom, if ever, excelled on the battle-field. As the men emerged from the forest into the valley before mentioned, they received a deadly volley at short range, which in a few seconds killed or disabled one-fourth their number. Halting without an order from me, and availing themselves of the shelter which the rocks afforded, they returned the fire. Such was their extreme exhaustion—having marched without interruption twenty-four miles to reach the battle-field and advanced at a double-quick step fully a mile to engage the enemy—that I hesitated for an instant to order them immediately forward. Perceiving very soon, however, that the enemy were giving away, I rushed forward, shouting to them to advance. It was with the greatest difficulty that I could make myself heard or understood above the din of battle. The order was, however, extended along the line, and was promptly obeyed; the men sprang forward over the rocks, swept the position and took possession of the heights, capturing forty or fifty prisoners around the battery and among the cliffs. Meanwhile the enemy had put a battery in position on a terrace of the mountain to our right, which opened on us an enfilading fire of grape and spherical case shot. A sharp fire of small arms was also opened from the same direction. This was not destructive, however, owing to the protection afforded by the rocks. At this critical moment General Benning's Brigade of Georgians advanced gallantly into action; his extreme right lapping upon my left, swarmed over the cliffs and mingled with my men. It was now past 5 P. M.; the conflict continued to rage with great fury until dark. Again and again the enemy in great force attempted to dislodge us from the position and re-take the battery, in each case with signal failure and heavy loss.

[NOTE.—Colonel Perry's report is very accurate in almost every particular. He evidently witnessed the occupation of Little Round Top by the Federal troops, and alludes to Benning's Brigade as joining on his right at this time. This was at the time that brigade moved through the gorge. The fatal mistake of allowing the enemy to occupy the woods on our left was turned to good account by them, they making use of it as a rallying point.—J. E. S.]

Report of Brig.-Gen. J. B. Robertson, Confederate States Army, commanding brigade:

* * * "Understanding before the action commenced that the attack on our part was to be general, and that the force of General Law's center was to advance simultaneously with us on my immediate left, and seeing at once that a mountain held by the enemy in heavy force, with artillery, to the right of General Law's centre was the key to the enemy's left, I abandoned the pike, and closed on General Law's left. This caused some separation of my regiments, which was remedied as promptly as the numerous stone and rail fences that intersected the field through which we were advancing would allow. As we advanced through this field, for half a mile, we were exposed to a heavy and destructive fire of canister, grape, and shell from six pieces of their artillery on the mountain alluded to, and the same number on a commanding hill but a short distance to the left of the mountain, and from the enemy's sharpshooters from behind the numerous rocks, fences and houses in the field. * * * Lieutenant-Colonel Work, with the 1st Texas Regiment, having pressed forward to the crest of the hill and driven the enemy from his battery, I ordered him to the left to the relief and support of Colonel Manning, directing Major Bass, with two companies, to hold the hill while Colonel Worth with the rest of the regiment went to Colonel Manning's relief. With this assistance, Colonel Manning drove the enemy back and entered the woods after him, when the enemy re-occupied the hill and his batteries in Colonel Work's front, from which Colonel Work again drove him." * * *

Report of Maj. J. P. Bane, 4th Texas:

* * * "Advancing at double-quick, we soon met the enemy's skirmishers, who occupied a skirt of thick undergrowth about one-quarter of a mile from the base of the cliffs, upon which the enemy had a battery playing upon us with the most deadly effect." * * *

Report of Lieut.-Col. William S. Shepherd, 2d Georgia:

* * * "Just before reaching its position in line, the regiment advanced by the right flank through an open field, under a heavy fire from the enemy's artillery, which was posted on a commanding position. * * * Before advancing in line of battle, the command was permitted to rest a few moments. The 2d Georgia composed the right, and, with the 17th Georgia the right wing of Benning's Brigade. Soon the order to advance was given, when the entire regiment moved forward in splendid order until it came to a deep gorge, where the nature of the ground was such that it was impossible to preserve an alignment; but, notwithstanding the rocks, undergrowth and the deadly fire of the enemy, the officers and men of this regiment moved forward with dauntless courage, driving the enemy before them, and it did not halt until they saw they were

some distance in advance of their line, and beyond a rocky eminence on the left, which had been previously held by the enemy. Here the regiment made a stand and fought as gallantly as men could fight, and did not yield an inch of ground, but repulsed several charges made by the enemy, who were protected by a battery and a hill lined with sharpshooters." * * *

Report of Col. W. C. Hodges, 17th Georgia:

* * * "The 2d and 17th Georgia regiments formed the right wing of Benning's Brigade ; and, after being formed in line facing the enemy under a murderous fire of artillery, *ably served*, and volleys of musketry, dashed forward gallantly and with impetuosity, until a four-gun battery of the enemy, from which we had received no little annoyance, was passed by the left of my regiment; and many of the officers and men, both of said battery and its support, composed in part of a detachment of the 4th Maine infantry, were captured and sent to the rear by the men of my command.

It is not intended in this statement to set up any exclusive claim to the capture of the battery, which, having had its support stripped from it in the manner indicated, remained at the command of the brigade until removed under cover of night. The position of my regiment in relation to this battery proves its instrumentality in the valuable capture." * * *

[NOTE.—No officers or enlisted men, save Broderick, were captured from the Battery.—J. E. S.]

Report of Col. J. Waddell, 17th Georgia:

* * * "The enemy's guns commanded a considerable portion of this distance and opened a heavy fire of shell upon us for more than a mile of the way. About 5 P. M., having reached the intended point, we advanced in line of battle to assault, the regiment moving in excellent order and spirit. We had not advanced far before it was ascertained that there was a considerable space intervening between Law's and Robertson's Brigades, unoccupied by any Confederate troops save very few belonging to the 1st Texas Regiment. Near to the center of this comparatively unoccupied ground, upon a steep, rocky, rugged hill, the enemy had posted a battery of six guns from which a destructive and vigorous fire was poured in our ranks. To cover this ground and to support Brigadier-General (J. B.) Robertson, who was pressed severely at the time, a left and oblique movement was made and continued until the 20th Regiment fronted this battery, when the brigade was ordered to advance forward. The order was obeyed by the regiment with promptness and alacrity, and the charge upon the hill and battery executed courageously and successfully. In the space of fifteen minutes the hill was carried and three ten-pounder Parrott guns captured. They were brought off that night and the next day turned against the enemy in that terrible artillery fight. Some twenty-five prisoners were captured and sent to the rear, some of whom aided our wounded in getting to the hospital. Three regiments, viz.: the 99th Pennsylvania, 124th New York and the 4th Maine were represented in the persons of the prisoners." * * *

[NOTE.—These official reports of Confederate officers in command of troops who were engaged in the capture of the three guns, strongly corroborate every statement made by me. When Hood's Division began the advance, Law's Brigade was on his right, with Benning's in rear, while Robertson's Brigade was on his left, with Anderson's in rear, reaching the woods on our left. Law's Brigade moved to their right to ascend Round Top while Benning moved to their left to fill the opening between Law's left and Robertson's right. This movement placed Benning's Brigade across the gorge, forming a line in the order indicated in the sketch, to wit: *Law's, Benning's, Robertson's, Anderson's.* Benning's Brigade, with right in front, moved up through the gorge by the flank (see diagram). This explains how the ridge was flanked; the two guns were run forward by hand to dispute Benning's advance.—J. E. S.]

CHAPTER XI

Letters from Participants in the Battle Referring to the Part Taken by the Battery.

To CONCLUDE, I will add a few quotations from letters, etc.

Correspondence with the New York *Herald*, in 1864, relating to the battle of Gettysburg, July 2, 1863, signed "Historicus":

* * * "The critical moment had now arrived; the enemy's movements indicated their purpose to seize Round Top hill; and this in their possession, General Longstreet would have had easy work in cutting up our left wing. To prevent this disaster, Sickles waited no longer for orders from General Meade, but directed General Hobart Ward's brigade and Smith's Battery (4th New York to secure that vital position." * * *

A letter written by Major Thomas W. Bradley, 124th New York Volunteers, and published in the *National Tribune*, February 4, 1886:

"Smith's Battery has not received in history full credit for the heroic and valuable work done by its members at Gettysburg. I was at that time 1st sergeant of Company "H," 124th New York. I saw the Battery come down Rock Run Glen. The guns were unlimbered at the foot of Rock Ridge and hauled up the steep acclivity into position amid the rocks on its crest, and the Battery was soon engaged in a hot duel with the rebel batteries on the heights beyond the "peach orchard." Under cover of the Confederate fire, Longstreet's Corps, massed in battle lines eight or ten deep, moved in confident, rapid attack on our position. The Battery changed from shell to canister, and, working as I never saw gunners work before or since, tore gap after gap through the ranks of the advancing foe. All this time the men were exposed to the direct fire of Longstreet's Sharpshooters, and his front line. Every round of ammunition had to be carried from the foot of the ridge, the Battery keeping up a well-directed fire until the enemy was at the base of the heights and the guns could no longer be depressed to reach him. Then knowing that greatly superior force would overwhelm us and capture the guns unless checked, Colonel Ellis of the 124th, after a few rapid words with Major Cromwell, ordered a charge. It was immediately responded to and as quickly repulsed. It was again made in the face of a withering fire that left killed and wounded two-fifths of the regiment. Flanked at the Devil's Den by the turning of our line at that point, we were swept from the position, and the crest and guns were for a brief time in possession of the enemy. Meanwhile Captain Smith had removed horses, caissons and ammunition, rendering the guns useless to the enemy, whose hold on the position was so short that he could not remove them. * * * Longstreet's determined charge, now so famous in history, was so dauntlessly met by our single line of battle on the crest of Rock Ridge, his force so terribly broken by the merciless fire of Smith's canister and the fierce grapple amid the rocks of Devil's Den. * * * The foregoing account is my recollection of Gettysburg, July 2, 1863. It may be faulty; it was more than twenty-two years ago, and I was but nineteen years of age then. The business cares and thoughts of an active life have come in between. I was seriously wounded in the second charge and my memories of the last part of the contest are confused with the agony of wounds, of being trampled under foot, carried and placed helplessly beside a rock on the other slope between both fires, hoping as I lay there that I might live long enough to see our side win, which I did, thank God! I recovered and returned to duty. During the last of my service I was a major and aide-de-camp on the staff of the Third Division, Second Corps. This Division was formed by the remnant of the old Third Corps left alive after Gettysburg. I managed to get 'plugged' a couple of times after that and yet see and take part in some pretty active fighting, but I never saw such a gallant rush 'into the jaws of Hell' as was made by our little regiment that July day, or a Battery worked and fought with such coolness and skill, such tireless devotion, and with such terrible havoc to the enemy. * * * Without that charge and the work of Smith's Battery, our left would have been more seriously turned; but now, in the light of after experience, as I think of it, what a mad act it was. Our regiment—a mere handful, at that—with no order back of its Colonel, charging from its base in line of battle to lock arms with Longstreet. This good it did, it gave pluck and steadiness to the men at our left, who were needing it and who fought like heroes, as the slaughter-house in the Den abundantly attested."

The following is an extract from a private letter (to Captain James E. Smith of Smith's 4th New York Battery, now of Washington, D. C.) from A. W. Tucker, 124th New York, Dallas City, Pa., author of the article on the "Orange Blossoms" in the *National Tribune* of January 21, 1886:

"You are right in your conclusions why we did not bring off your guns. Your one supposition that we were too few in numbers when relieved, is partially correct; and again that we did not occupy the same ground as when the fight opened. By the loss occasioned during the battle, we had kept closing to the right, so that when relieved, my company, which was on the left of the regiment, was where the right of the regiment was when the fight opened. Hence, we were at least one hundred yards to the right of your guns. I do not know what troops were in the vicinity of the guns, but think it must have been the 99th Pennsylvania. I am glad to be able to clear up the mystery why we failed to bring off your guns." * * *.

Extract from a letter published in *National Tribune* January 21, 1886, by A. W. Tucker, Company "B," 124th New York, Dallas City, Pa.:

* * * "A short time previous, Smith's Battery went into position about two rods to the left and front of Company "B" of our regiment. I was where I could see every movement and hear every order. It had hardly taken position before a rebel battery on the Emmittsburg ridge opened on it. Smith's Battery responded in gallant style. The rebels then brought two more batteries of six guns each in position, nearly in front of our regiment and not half a mile distant. Their efforts to silence Smith's Battery made our position almost untenable. Our Colonel (Ellis) moved us by the right flank into the woods on which our right rested. I judge he thought, after he had got us in there that instead of the woods being a protection they made our next position more hazardous than the one we had just abandoned. We were soon moved by the left flank back to our old position, Company "B" resting within a few feet of Smith's Battery. During all this time the cannonading was going on incessantly. * * * It lasted for about an hour. There were some several casualties in our regiment from the enemy's shells. About 3 P. M. the cannonading seemed to stop by mutual

J HARVEY HANFORD.

consent, as though for a breathing spell; but it was of short duration. At once we could see emerge from the woods along the Emmittsburg road a deployed rebel skirmish line; within supporting distance was a long line of battle extending in either direction as far as the eye could reach. It was followed by a second and third line, each in supporting distance. It was at this particular time that Smith's Battery did splendid service. The guns were worked to their utmost, every order was given in a clear, distinct tone that could be heard above the tumult. I heard the gunners directed to use five and six second fuse, and when the gunners reported that the case shot and shrapnel were all gone, I heard the order, 'Give them shell! Give them solid shot! Damn them, give them anything.'

"The guns were worked until the ammunition was gone, several of the Battery men had been shot and the rebels were within pistol range." * * *

A letter published in the *National Tribune* December 23, 1885, from J. Harvey Hanford, Unionville, Orange County, New York, formerly of the 124th New York:

To the Editor:
"In a late issue of the *National Tribune* you invite a minute description of an active private soldier's experience on the battlefield of Gettysburg. I will try to give you a part of mine. I was 2d sergeant of Company "B" 124th N. Y. Vols., and together with the rest of the regiment and others reached the vicinity of Gettysburg at 8.30 P. M., July 1, 1863. We lay down in an open field, with orders to sleep on our arms, and not take off an article of clothing or any of our accouterments. This was hard sauce after such a march as we had had; but soldier-like, we had to take it out in grumbling. Early in the morning of the 2d we got our breakfast, and were then formed in line of battle behind a stone wall—an excellent position we thought. Not

long after the order 'Forward, march!' was given, and after crossing one or two fields we came to the famous wheat-field—and, by the way, it was the finest I ever saw, the wheat breast-high and ready to cut—but we marched through and over it in line of battle, and on looking back not a stock could be found, for it was all trodden out of sight. When nearly through the wheat-field the order was given, 'By the left flank, march!' and when halt was sounded, I being the extreme left man in the regiment, I found myself on the rocks at Devil's Den. A battery of guns, commanded by Captain Smith, was soon in our midst. On this spot we lounged for some time, taking it easy. Our signal corps was a little to the left and rear of us, on Little Round Top. Presently a shell came shrieking and bursting near us; we needed no order or invitation to get behind the rocks, but did so at once. Then followed the usual cannonading until the infantry of the Confederates got so close as to pick off all our gunners. Then shone out the bravery of Captain Smith. When he had not men enough left to man the guns, he would come to us and ask and beg of us to help him fire them. Then he would run back to the guns and do what he could, and then back to us, and, with tears in his eyes would say: 'For God's sake, men, don't let them take my guns away from me!' (Twenty-two years ago, yet I can see his looks and hear his voice.) O, how I would like to see him and thank him for what he then did, and if this meets his eye I would like to have him write to me. We were ordered to charge, and charge we did, driving the enemy back to the foot of the hill. We made four charges that afternoon, and held our ground until out of ammunition.

"A little incident happened after our last charge. As I was kneeling behind a rock and loading my gun, Lieutenant Dennison, of the next company, had picked up a gun, and, there being a rock to my left hand, he jumped over my arms and caught his toe in my ramrod, bending it so I could not use it. I scolded him for it, but looking around I picked up another one. The Lieutenant squatted behind the rock, and was in the act of firing his gun when he was struck by a bullet in the leg. With a cry, 'I've got it, I've got it,' he started for the rear, but before getting far another one struck him, so he had to be carried off the field. While I was behind the rock I was struck four times, but not seriously. My attention was all the time on an open space, apparently like a pair of bars, in the stone wall at the foot of the hill, behind which the enemy had taken cover. Into this I did most of my firing, as it was all the time crowded full of men. After using all my ammunition I went back to and over the brow of the hill, and there saw we were about to be relieved by other troops. What there was left of us passed through the ranks of the fresh troops, and we made our way to the rear. Our regiment, which was raised in Orange County, N. Y., and was by its Colonel (Ellis) called the 'Orange Blossoms,' with the aid of citizens of the county, have erected a nice monument on the ground where we fought. This was all the fighting we were in at this battle, as we were so badly cut up as to be hardly a show of a regiment.

"I saw in a paper some time ago that our twin regiment, the 86th New York, which was on our right, were going to erect a monument on the ground, and I hope they will. I think when the battle commenced on the second day I was the last man on the extreme left of the army. I know that at one time the enemy had passed our left flank and were enfilading us; but it was only for a minute or two. Our regiment holds a reunion each year, this year in Middletown, Orange County, N. Y., September 23, 1885. I wish we could see a good number of the 86th New York with us.

"J. HARVEY HANFORD,
"*2d Sergt. Co. 'B,' 124th N. Y.,*
"*Unionville, Orange Co., N. Y.*"

Extract from a letter published in Orange County *Press*, August 10, 1883.

* * * "The field and woods are as they were except the wheat. I could tell where the Battery stood in front of us that did such fearful execution. And how often do I think of the Captain's bravery and his appeals to us not to let his guns be taken from him." (J. HARVEY HANFORD, 124*th* N. Y. Vols., "*Orange Blossoms.*")

Extract of letter from Elijah Walker, Colonel 4th Maine, Somerville, Mass.

* * * "We took position on the left, our right connecting with or near to the 124th New York. A part of my command was to the right and a part to the left of Smith's Battery, and it was the left of the army at that time. I was ordered farther to the left, into the Devil's Den, leaving Smith's Battery exposed, against which I remonstrated; but Captain Smith said he could take care of his guns and did not want my help. I moved to the left, across the Den, to the woods, with my right forming a skirmish line near the largest works, and my left in line of battle near the woods, or bushes, at the foot of Round Top. We were attacked by a skirmish-line in the Den, and on our left flank by a force from the woods. To meet these latter, the left of my line was refused and their attack was repulsed. I then found that the enemy was coming over Smith's guns in the rear of my right. Here was a desperate struggle. We fell back, fixed bayonets, charged, re-took Smith's guns and established our line in rear of them, with my right near the 124th New York. My line thus formed, my left was exposed, and for a few minutes we had a hot time there, but the 99th Pennsylvania Reserves came up in our rear and formed on our left, swinging back and facing the Den; but they did not go beyond the high ground, and the 4th Maine was the only regiment that had a line of men in the Devil's Den, July 2, 1863, between the hours of 3 and 6 o'clock P. M., all stories that have been told to the contrary notwithstanding. We held the line until the entire brigade fell back, when I was led to the rear by two of my men. My horse had been killed, and I had lost the use of one leg."

"*Capt. James E. Smith.*

"*Dear Comrade:* In compliance with your request that I send you a brief statement of my recollection of the part taken by a section of your Battery, the 4th New York Independent, in the battle of Gettysburg, from my personal observation, I take pleasure in furnishing my evidence as to the important and signal service rendered by you in that memorable engagement, from my point of view.

"As preliminary, however, I will state that the Fifth Corps, of which my regiment, the 44th New York, formed a part, reached the Gettysburg battle-field on the morning of July 2d, 1863, and was stationed on the right of the Union line. In the afternoon General Sykes in command of the Corps was ordered to protect the left of the line, and about 4 P. M. we were moved rapidly to the left, where Sickles was engaged with the Third Corps in meeting and repelling the assault of Longstreet. When we reached the wheat-field we were halted and formed in line of battle. At this time General Warren, who was then a member of General Meade's staff, rode up and urged the necessity of seizing "Little Round Top," a rocky hill to the left and rear of our then line of battle. General Sykes, appreciating the importance of Warren's suggestion, immediately detached the Third Brigade of the First Division, consisting of the 83d Pennsylvania, 20th Maine, 16th Michigan, and 44th New York, to which latter regiment I had the honor to belong; and we were at once turned over to General Warren and double-quicked to the rear of Little Round Top, fronted and moved over the crest in the line of battle to a position a little more than half way down the slope, the 16th Michigan occupying the right, the 44th New York and 83d Pennsylvania the centre, and the 20th Maine the left. In front of Little Round Top was a wood, beyond which was a wide, open space of field, on the further edge of which appeared another piece of woods. As we moved forward over the crest of Little Round Top, I noticed three heavy lines of battle of the enemy emerging from the farther woods and advancing on our front. At the foot of Little Round Top, and extending around our right, was a ravine or gorge leading out of the woods in our front and to our right and rear, beyond which was a rocky ridge or spur occupied by a battery then in action, apparently forming the left of the Union line prior to our occupancy of Little Round Top.

"We had hardly obtained our position in line of battle, when our skirmishers were rapidly driven in by the advancing enemy, and a heavy assault was made by them on the centre of our line by Hood's division of Texans, belonging to Longstreet's Corps, and the battle for a time raged with terrific ferocity, neither side giving an inch. Suddenly about this time we heard the whirr of grape, canister and shell over our heads, and learned that Hazlett's Battery "D," 5th Regular Artillery, had been hauled up by hand and placed in position on the crest of Little Round Top, in our rear. The combined fire from our line and from this Battery caused the rebel line in our front to recoil and surge toward the right, and we were relieved from anxiety as to our immediate front, and enabled to turn our attention to the right, where our line had apparently given away and the rebels were surging over the rocky ridge beyond the ravine occupied by the battery already mentioned as in action at the time we took the position. At this time I noticed in the ravine at the foot of the hill, immediately on our right, two guns, apparently without any support, being rapidly loaded and fired into a column of rebels advancing up the ravine, in the direction of the guns, without regular formation, but in a heavy mass composed of several regiments, judging from the number of stands of colors in close proximity, and apparently intent on capturing the guns. From the more elevated position occupied by our line we were better enabled to see this advancing force than the officer in command of the guns, and believing he was not fully aware of his perilous position, I felt much anxiety for the safety of the guns, and my special attention was attracted by the gallant manner in which they were handled and fought; the rapidity with which they were loaded and fired, and the terrible execution wrought by their charges of grape and canister on the head of the advancing column of the enemy. More especially was my attention attracted to the officer in command, who immediately after each discharge rushed out beyond the volume of smoke from his guns for the purpose of observing the effect of the shot, and the position and proximity of the enemy, when he would rush back, seize the trail of a gun, slew it around for the purpose of directing the fire a little to the right or left, and send another charge of canister down the ravine to his front. Meantime we were delivering a galling fire into the flank of this rebel column, which apparently paid little attention to us, being intent on capturing the guns and turning our flank. From the effect of our fire and the terrible storm of grape and canister poured into the head of the column at close range from the two guns in the ravine, they went down in scores; at times two or three stands of colors seemed to go to the ground at once, but they were immediately picked up, and the column, or more properly, mass of rebels, for they had lost all regular formation, surged steadily forward until they were enveloped by the smoke of the last discharge of these two guns in their very faces. At the same time the guns were enveloped from the right and flank by the rebel line that rushed over the rocky ridge on the right, and the gunners were compelled to abandon the guns and were forced back through the opening in our line to our right and rear.

"At this time a portion of the 16th Michigan, forming the right of our brigade, was forced back to the crest of the hill, and our brigade commander, General Vincent, was mortally wounded.

"I did not know then to what battery the two guns belonged or who commanded them, but the brave fight they made without support, in the very teeth of the advancing enemy, and the gallant conduct of their commanding officer, are features so forcibly impressed upon my memory as never to be effaced.

"Some years after the war (1888) when on a visit to Gettysburg battle-field with a comrade of my regiment, D. W. Harrington, now, and for some years past, Chief of the Division of Accounts, U. S. Treasury Department, we were looking over the ground and recalling incidents of the battle, when I referred to that related above concerning *the fight* made by these two guns in the ravine at the foot of the hill on our right, and remarked that I would give considerable to know the name of the officer commanding those guns, and to what battery they belonged.

"At the time of this conversation with Comrade Harrington, I noticed a fine appearing, military looking gentleman near us who seemed much interested in my relation of the incident and who immediately introduced himself as Captain James E. Smith, who had the honor to command a Battery, the 4th New York, to which he assured me the section referred to belonged, as well as the guns on the rocky ridge to the right of the ravine, which I had noticed in action at the time we went into position on Little Round Top, and which he informed me were captured when the enemy gained the ridge.

"It is needless to say that that gentleman was yourself, and the acquaintance made with you that day has continued, and has always been regarded by me as one of the pleasant episodes of my life. In my own humble opinion, the service performed by you with those two guns was of vital importance, at a critical juncture of the battle, when the weight and force of the rebel onslaught had shattered our line on the right of Round Top, and success was trembling in the balance; when the holding of the left with tenacity and determination until the victorious enemy could be checked, and the gap closed, meant victory or defeat to our army in the event of failure. Your services at that critical point and time can not, in my opinion, be over-estimated, and the record you made on that day is one of which any soldier may well feel proud.

"It is generally conceded by writers on the battle, that had the line on Round Top held by our brigade given away at that time, the result would have been far different, and in my opinion, the obstinate fight made by you with the two guns in the ravine on the right of that line, which had already begun to give back, checked the rebel advance, and afforded time to meet and drive them back, and thus enabled us to hold our position, which possibly we would have been compelled to abandon, had the column checked by you had a few moments more time to have got through the opening in our line.

"I make this statement in justice to you in view of my personal observation, because of the fact that official reports appear to be confined more especially to the operations of that portion of your Battery engaged earlier in the action, on the rocky ridge farther to the right and front, and to have overlooked this section farther to the rear in the ravine, and failed to recognize the important service performed by it, and because I believe your natural modesty impelled you to omit from your official report anything that might be construed as egotistical, and hence failed to do you full justice.

I am sincerely your friend and comrade,

WM. J. JOHNSTON,
Late 44th N. Y., 3rd Brigade, 1st Div., 5th Corps.
ATTORNEY-AT-LAW, 629 F STREET,
WASHINGTON, D. C.

Extract from a history of the Fifth Army Corps:

* * * "The whole Confederate line was sweeping from out the woods in which it had formed, far outflanking the left of the Third Corps, and, where Smith's Battery, in air and almost unsupported, on the rocks of the Devil's Den, gallantly waited its doom, and between that left and the Round Tops the way to the death of the Nation lay invitingly open to the confidently advancing enemy. * * * General Sykes discovering the undefended gorge upon the left of the Third Corps line and the inadequacy of the support given to Smith's Battery, he suggested to General Birney to close his division line upon the Battery, while he (Sykes) would fill the gap which would be made by the movement with troops from the Fifth Corps." * * *

[NOTE.—The history by the Comte de Paris has much to say upon this subject, but as it is based upon the facts already introduced, it is thought to be unnecessary to quote therefrom. The same can be said of the letters recently published in the *Century Magazine.*—J. E. S.]

CHAPTER XII

Remarks and Criticisms

It will be noticed that several allusions have been made to the protection furnished by the large boulders which covered the ground in the vicinity of the ridge. I can bear witness that these rocks served to protect, and no doubt, preserve the lives of many during that battle; to their friendly shelter may be attributed the small loss, comparatively speaking, sustained by the Battery. Not that the men dodged nor neglected their duty; this was by no means the case, but the close proximity of the boulders to the guns made it possible for the cannoneers to step behind them during the discharge of their respective pieces. I believe in this manner the enemy's artillery was cheated, for notwithstanding their excellent and accurate aim, not one man in the Battery was touched by their numerous shot and shells which landed on the crest, or the countless missiles sent whizzing through the air, as the result of larger metal coming in contact with the rocks.

The position occupied by the monument erected by the State of New York is not upon the ground where the guns were stationed; its location is in a hole and indicates that the line of the Battery's fire was in the direction of the "peach orchard."

I am not prepared to say that this unfortunate position

of the monument, intended to commemorate the position held by the guns, was the result of design or misapprehension; certain it is, my efforts were exerted to the extent of my ability, backed by such eminent authority as the late Gen. H. J. Hunt, Chief of Artillery of the Army of the Potomac, and Col. George E. Randolph, Chief of Third Corps Artillery, not to mention the rank and file of the "Orauge Blossoms," who were interested spectators for more than one hour, as they lay within a few feet of the guns during the artillery duel. The only thing I could do was to enter my earnest protest. In the future the monument may be properly located; at least such is my hope. The following resolution will show that the Battery Association has done all that it could to have this rectified:

(Copy.)

"HEADQUARTERS
"4th N. Y. IND. BATTERY ASSOCIATION,
"781 EIGHTH AVENUE,
"NEW YORK CITY, *October* 31st, 1888.

"*Major Geo. W. Cooney, Secretary.*

"*Dear Major:* I have the honor to submit the following extract from minutes of meeting of above-mentioned Association, held on Thursday evening, October 30, 1888:

"'*Whereas*, in the judgment of several members of the 4th N. Y. Independent Battery Association (who participated in the Battle of Gettysburg, Pa., on July 2, 1863, and who have subsequently visited the scene of the conflict), the location of the Battery Monument erected thereon is not historically correct; Therefore, be it

"'*Resolved*, That the Honorable Board of New York State Commissioners of Gettysburg Monuments be most respectfully petitioned to change the location of the Monument, in accordance with views previously expressed by

"'Gen. HUNT, Chief of Artillery, A. of P.
"'Col. RANDOLPH, Chief of Artillery, 3d Corps.
"'Capt. JAS. E. SMITH, Commanding Battery.'
" Yours very truly,
" (Signed) JAS. S. FRASER."
"*Acting Secretary.*"

During the 25th Anniversary of the battle, July 2, 1888, the late General Hunt visited Devil's Den in my company; standing on the same large rock we occupied together twenty-five years before (while the guns on our right were actively replying to those of the Confederates) he said: "Captain, get a painter and have painted upon this rock the fact that your left piece rested within a few feet, and to the north, of this point, and you will have a historical monument located upon the ground occupied by your guns on this ridge. If you had placed your pieces down where the monument stands, I would have placed you in arrest for incompetency. It is not flattering to my intelligence as an artillerist to infer that I did countenance such a position while a better one was to be had."

I will add that General Hunt repeated the substance of the above conversation to General Sickles at dinner that very day, and subsequently, in a letter to me, which I filed with the Secretary of the New York Monument Committee. It is not my purpose to furnish the cause—I merely state the facts.

It may be well to add that when General Hunt and I met in 1888, we talked over and explained several matters not made clear before, by walking over the ground and pointing out the different positions occupied by the Battery, etc. The General expressed his astonishment at having failed to realize the importance of the service rendered by the two pieces in rear of the crest. "I never could," said he, "understand about those two guns, but now you have made everything very plain. If I had known this before writing my *Century* article, it could have been used to good advantage. But never mind, I have been asked to write a history of the artillery, and may do so; in the meantime you can furnish me with a supplemental statement to your official report, which, by the way, is very short, and, in my opinion, does not cover the ground fully."

One word more before I leave this field. Many histories have been written by various authors whose information was obtained from the best and most reliable sources, much of it, presumably, from eye-witnesses. That of the Compte de Paris is, beyond doubt, the most exhaustive and impartial as well as the most correct. In no other history, so far as I know, has the slightest reference been made to the Battery, notwithstanding this undeniable fact, that the Battery opened the battle at Devil's Den and closed it just in rear of the ridge, so far as the troops of the Third Corps were concerned.

Without a desire to appear conspicuous, I assert now for the first time publicly, that I was the *very last* commissioned officer, and, I believe, the last person, to withdraw from the Federal left, occupied by and attached to Ward's Brigade. I arrive at this conclusion in this manner, to wit: I sent every man, horse and carriage into the woods on a road leading to the "wheat-field," following in rear until the woods were passed. Those who remained behind me were disabled and were beyond the ridge, then held by the enemy.

I allude to the ground in front and west of Little Round Top, where the left of the Third Corps fought until relieved by the presence of the Fifth Corps on the summit of Little Round Top. For not one moment of the four long hours consumed on the ridge and at the position a few rods in rear, was my attention diverted from the work before us. Every movement of the enemy was closely observed, the panorama lay before me like a map. I believed then as I do now, that my command had done nobly, and that their efforts would be duly recognized. I believed then, as I do now, that our position was wrested from us by men equally brave and determined, superior only in point of numbers. But time passed from days to weeks and from weeks to months, and so on into long years without the scantiest evidence in the way of recognition. I became careless and made up my mind to forget that the Battery had been engaged in this battle.

At last, twenty-two years after the conflict, an enlisted man who served in the ranks of the "Orange Blossoms" made honorable mention of the Battery (see J. Harvey Hanford's letter), and I am proud to know there are other men, too, now living who can testify to the conduct of the Battery and who have not forgotten the danger shared on the rock-bound crest of Devil's Den. At this time the Rebellion Records had not been published.

Extract from a letter written by General Hunt in 1883 in response to one asking why the Battery had not been credited with having rendered some service at Gettysburg July 2, 1863:

WASHINGTON, D. C., *August* 9, 1883.

* * * "I do not wonder at your feeling sore because little or no mention has been made of your Battery. When the war closed all official papers were taken in charge by the War Department, and carefully locked up where none but the initiated had access to them. * * * I remember that your Battery occupied a position cut off from the general view by a strip of woods. There was no Corps Commander there to be boomed, consequently, no newspaper correspondent. * * * Your Battery imposed a delay on Hood's troops at Devil's Den, which gave time to Warren to hasten forward defenders for Little Round Top, which, it is claimed, was lost by the enemy by less than five minutes, hence the importance of your fight at Devil's Den, of which little or no notice has been taken. They did things strangely in those days."

Extract from endorsement made by General Hunt, Soldier's Home, Washington, February 23, 1886:

"Captain J. E. Smith commanded the 4th New York Battery, Third Corps, Army of the Potomac. * * * At the Battle of Gettysburg he greatly distinguished himself and his Battery, *under my personal* observation, in the advanced position on the left of the Third Corps line.

"His Battery was posted by him on Devil's Den and maintained its position so long as a man was left to protect it."

From a letter to General Sheridan:

* * * "Captain Smith, late of the 4th New York Battery, was an excellent officer and greatly distinguished himself at Gettysburg, where his Battery, alone and but feebly supported, bore the first assault of Hood's Division on Devil's Den, in front of Round Top in the battle of the second day—(Sickles)."

There is nothing on record from the pen of Major-General D. E. Sickles, who commanded the Corps until he fell on the evening of the second day, but I have many assurances of his high opinion of the Battery and its services at Gettysburg, as the following indicates:

Extract from a letter to the Secretary of the Department of the Interior:

* * * "At the battle of Gettysburg, where the 4th New York Independent Battery is recognized by historians for its brilliant record."

Extract from a letter to the Secretary of War:

* * * "Captain Smith's conduct at Gettysburg in the defense of Round Top, at a critical moment on July 2, 1863, attracted my personal attention and was strongly commended by me on the field."

General Sickles has been severely criticised for advancing his command as he did on the morning of the 2d of July, 1863. Having served in the Third Corps under this distinguished officer (part of the time at headquarters as Chief of Artillery) I may be pardoned for here referring to this controversy.

I have noticed that those who shed their blood, or who fought in the ranks of this gallant and well-tried old Corps, on the advanced line, have found no fault with their Corps Commander. They know that they were never ordered forward while he remained in the rear. They remember that the old Corps flag, representing where their commander was to be found, was ever in sight, and that he fell, desperately wounded, right in the midst of the men who were struggling to resist the onslaught of Longstreet's overwhelming legions.

I will not presume to place my opinion as to the merits of the disputed position beside that of such high authorities as Generals Grant and Sheridan, who coincided in the view that "the advanced position was the only one to fight on." I have undoubted authority for stating that General Grant fully endorsed General Sickles's course, and refer to the copy of a letter, given below, from Gov. A. J. Curtin, repeating the substance of a conversation he had with General Sheridan on this subject. This should be sufficient to vindicate the wisdom and foresight of the one man who keenly realized the critical situation of the Federal left, and who had the nerve to meet the threatened danger with an inadequate force.

But he did not take upon himself the responsibility of this movement without consulting and endeavoring to secure the sanction of General Meade. The latter, however, seemed to attach slight importance to Sickles's urgent appeals, and appeared to think that the danger of any attack upon our left was too remote to be seriously considered. But the result proved that Sickles was right, and impartial history will accord him the justice and the honor due to his military genius.

The following is the letter above referred to:

"BELLEFONTE, PA., *October* 18, 1889.
"*Major-General Dan'l. E. Sickles,*
"*New York City.*

"*My dear General:* I repeated to you a conversation I had with General Sheridan before his death and after his examination of the field at Gettysburg and a full study of the strategy of both armies, and at your request wrote a letter to you, which I had supposed you had received until we met at Gettysburg in September.

"General Sheridan did not hesitate to say to me without disrespect to other officers there, that the movements on the 2d of July were well advised and proper, and as it was the design of the enemy to turn the flank of the army, that the attack made at that time and under the circumstances, was very important to prevent their advance. I am very clear in my judgment as to the statement of the General, and inferred from what he said that were it not for the attack made on the 2d, the flank would likely have been turned.

"When last at Gettysburg, with my recollection of what the General said to me, I went over all the ground and made an examination, and with the historical reports of the battle was confirmed that the views of that distinguished officer are correct.

"You stated to me at Gettysburg that you never received my letter, and I then said to you that the fact that you had not acknowledged its receipt gave me no little surprise, but I am now happy to make this statement and explanation, as surely justice should be done to you and all other men who bore so active and important a part in that long and terrible war.

"I remain as ever, truly your friend,
"(Signed.)   A. G. CURTIN,"

CHAPTER XIII

Poetic Tributes to the Battery

CAPT. JACK CRAWFORD, widely known as the "Poet-Scout," the author of the following spirited poem, needs no introduction to the American people. With his splendid Army record when a boy, his subsequent fame as Chief of Scouts for General Crook in his Indian campaigns, and his popularity as an off-hand speaker, he is a familiar figure throughout our country.

A FAMOUS BATTERY AND ITS DAY OF GLORY.

Respectfully Dedicated to the Gallant Survivors of Smith's 4th New York Independent Battery.

Sultrily dawned that summer day,
On the field where the waiting forces lay—
On the field of Gettysburg, where soon
The forms of the slain would be thickly strewn.
Up, like a ball of lurid fire,
The red sun mounted higher and higher,
Casting its shimmering, fiery rain

O'er the waving billows of ripening grain,
That waited the reaper's gleaming blade,
While near to its golden borders laid
A human harvest, with bated breath,
Awaiting the Reaper whose name is Death.
Eagerly gleamed each warrior eye—
Defiantly floated the flags on high—
One, the emblem of Union bands,
The other borne by disloyal hands.

Over the face of the peaceful farms
Echoed the clash of contending arms,
As, locked in the battle's dread embrace,
The smoke-grimed foemen stood face to face,
Hurling death to each other's ranks,
Blazing with fire from center to flanks,
Batteries belching their heated breath,
Over the carnival of death.

Up o'er a steep and rock-bound height,
Brave men toiled with unflagging might,
Dragging their guns to a point o'erhead,
Where hoofs of horses could never tread;
Up to a point that must be maintained,
Spite of the leaden shower that rained,
Spite of the flocks of screaming shell
That filled the air with the music of hell.
Onward, upward, those heroes pressed,
Till their guns peered over the rocky crest,
And hurled their volleys of death away,
To check the advancing tide of gray.
Perched on a rock the leader stood,

Watching the ranks of the chieftain Hood—
Watching the flight of his well-aimed shot—
Watching the carnage their mad speed wrought.
Advancing, recoiling, advancing again,
Came surging billows of gray-clad men,
Striving to occupy that crest,
Striving those deadly guns to wrest
From the grasp of that brave, heroic band,
That hurled forth death with unsparing hand.
Waving aloft his glittering sword,
Cheering his men with approving word,
Facing the storm with his loyal breast,
Stood he there on that boulder's crest.
Never a thought of undying fame,
Never a hope of an honored name
Nerved him to stand on that rocky height,
Where his form would the rebel shot invite.
Heard he only his chief's command:
"*Hold this height with unflinching hand!*
Never release it while you've got
A gunner left who can fire a shot!"
That the motive which held him there,
His form outlined in the smoke-tinged air—
No supporting force in his rear,
No reinforcements drawing near,
Naught but his own unaided band,
To hold that point from the rebel hand.

Longstreet's heroes of many a fight
Came charging up o'er the rocky height—
Came with their vengeful eyes awarm,
With the valor which nerves the warrior's arm,

Closing each rent the wild shells made
In their long gray ranks as if on parade.
Steadily, swiftly, like ocean tide,
They surged up the mountain's rocky side,
Until their disloyal feet were pressed
To the blood-stained soil of the mountain crest.
The gallant gunners were forced at last,
Like leaves in the teeth of a tempest blast,
To quit their places, but not for long,
For up from the rear, like a cheering song,
Came a slogan that caused their hearts to leap,
As the "Orange Blossoms" charged up the steep.
Backward the rebel ranks were hurled,
And Union's flag was again unfurled
O'er the guns (that were) for a moment lost;
Then gained again, at a fearful cost
To the daring warriors of Longstreet's Corps,
And again did their fierce, ear-deafening roar
Belch forth in chorus the song of death,
As the missiles sped from their fiery breath,
Thinning the ranks of the fleeing foe,
That reeled and staggered beneath the blow;
Nor cooled a throat of a brazen gun,
Till the storm had passed and the day was won.

A memory, now, of near three decades,
Are the scenes 'mid Gettysburg's hills and glades,
When the dawn of a summer day gave birth
To a roar of battle heard 'round the earth.
Few live who so nobly then did stand
To the guns of that gallant chief's command,

And low on a bed of ceaseless pain,
That hero-commander long has lain—
Lain unflinching as when he stood,
Watching the ranks of the dauntless Hood—
Lain with laboring, pain-clogged breath,
Calmly awaiting the call of Death.
Men who no brighter laurels wore
Have trodden the path to death before,
And a world has wept in distress most dire
When the looked-for tidings flashed o'er the wire,
And every city along their track
Was swarthed in emblems of sombre black,
And yet the grief of a world can not
Eclipse the sorrow of those who fought
With the gallant Smith on that fearful day,
When he held the disloyal hordes at bay—
No tears so warm as the comrade tears,
When the tidings will reach the comrade ears,
That he whose presence on that red field
Was an inspiration to them that steeled
Their valiant bosoms, and nerved their arms
To work in face of disloyal swarms,
Has passed from the scenes of earth away
To the gladsome light of Eternal Day.

CAPT. JACK CRAWFORD,
"The Poet Scout."

The author of the poem below is well known in Washington as a writer of graceful verse. He has published a volume of his fugitive pieces, entitled "Sprigs of Acacia," which is much admired.

"DEVIL'S DEN."

Gettysburg, July 2, 1863.

BY COMRADE SAMUEL ADAMS WIGGIN.

The day in matchless beauty dawned in peace,
The sun in glowing splendor wreathed the summer skies;
Its golden chariot with its smoking steeds
Passed the proud zenith of its path of light.
The air waxed hot and hotter still,
Until the heavens like molten brass became.
Fierce rays from torrid zones of living flame
Descended on the verdant vales and hills,
On serried columns of the hosts of war,
On dashing cavalry—Artillery's dread array—
The furious cohorts of the Boys in Gray.
Desperate, impetuous as a hope forlorn,
Right onward dashed the battalions of the South,
Hood's bravest legions—valorous sons of Mars,
Longstreet's artillery in battle's set array.
Upon the lofty crest of famous Devil's Den,
Perched the brave boys of New York Battery Four,
Sons of the Empire State, valiant and tried and true,
They faced the rushing foe and held the fatal pass
'Gainst overwhelming legions of the Boys in Gray.
Close by the old Fourth Maine and "Orange Blossoms" brave,

A living wall of grand, heroic souls,
That for the Nation's honor scorned the monster death,
In all his fearful forms of carnage, strife and blood,
They held the pass until the Boys in Blue,
On Little Round Top's crest, in mighty legions stood,
Massed in full force and eager for the fray,
They held the pass. They fought like heroes true;
Death and destruction swept the Southern lines;
The Devil's Den ablaze with fires of hell
Let loose the "Dogs of War" on the advancing foe,
With fangs of steel and scorching breath of flame,
Until the vale of Plum Run, battle's tide
Was piled with gasping heaps of mangled forms in gray.

A fearful, desperate fight of life and sudden death
For freedom and the Union's sacred cause;
'Gainst all the martial flower of chivalry's proud might,
Three hours they held the pass, then spiked the guns,
Fell back on Round Top—facing still the foe
And Gettysburg, that saved the Union fair,
Sheds lustre on those heroes banded there.

Smith's New York Independent Battery Four,
Won there on Devil's Den renown forevermore.
The "Old Fourth Maine" that to the rescue came,
Brave "Orange Blossoms" on the scroll of fame,
In golden characters are written there,
The precious heritage of noble heroes rare.
Crown them with fadeless wreaths—our pride and
    boast—
Deck their broad breasts with Stars of Freedom's host,
Walk softly where their dying comrades fell,

Loud let your glorious pæans for the living swell,
Room for the war-worn veterans true and bold,
Room for the noble boys fast growing old,
Honors and station, place and laurel crown
For heroes of that day of Gettysburg renown,
That saved the Nation and the Union sweet.
All hail the boys, the boys with way-worn feet,
The truest souls, the grandest hearts that beat,
All love and praise for Boys in Bonny Blue,
Our stalwart heroes, tender, brave and true.
No blot of shame, no missing radiant star,
Mars the dear flag they saved in Freedom's glorious war.
Rest on your laurels bright, a fearful fight you fought
With ransom of your blood the Nation's life was bought.

CHAPTER XIV

Back to Washington—Disbanded

THE Battery continued with the Third Corps until the army reached Boonsboro, Md. General Hunt then directed me to return to Frederick and turn over all the ordnance stores appertaining to the ten-pounder Parrotts, and then proceed to Washington and procure a battery of six light twelve-pounders—Napoleons.

Owing to the washing away of a culvert on the B. & O. R. R., I decided to make the trip during the night on horse-back. It was a long ride. The débris of burning forage wagons, destroyed by Mosby and his men, were numerous, but beyond a few sutlers who were trying to reach the army, we did not meet any one. At one point on the road we came upon four or five of these (sutlers) sleeping on long wooden benches on the porch of a country inn. I did not like to pass them without ascertaining who they were, therefore instructing Lieutenant Goodman, who accompanied me, to ride on one side of the orderly while I took the other, we dismounted, handed the reins to the orderly, and drew our revolvers, ready for use.

We approached from different directions, and on reaching the benches called on the sleepers to hold up their hands. Not being able to arouse them in this gentle manner, I took hold of and capsized a bench, when a comical scene occurred.

Every man jumped to his feet and stretched both hands as high as he could hold them. Explanations followed; they had taken us for Mosby's Guerillas, while we were in doubt as to the status of the sleepers.

Before leaving Frederick I directed Lieutenant McLean to march to Sandy Hook, Md., with the men and horses, where I expected to rejoin the army. Being detained some days in Washington, D. C., I found upon my arrival at Sandy Hook that the army had crossed the Potomac two days before. The bridge was still in position and I proposed to follow, but General Lockwood, then in command of Harper's Ferry, telegraphed the situation to General Halleck, and I was ordered back to Washington. Transportation by rail over the single track to the Capital was difficult to obtain and uncertain in its results, blockades and smash ups being of daily occurrence. So it was decided to send the Battery by canal, in charge of Lieutenant McLean. A number of empty boats were pressed into service, the guns, carriages and baggage loaded, tow-lines improvised from prolonges, and the Battery horses, steeds that "had smelt the battle from afar"—and near, too—took the places of the patient mule on the tow-path, and the company gayly started for Washington, some eighty miles away.

The sturdy animals bent to their unaccustomed work, and as the flotilla pulled around a bend and the luxuriant foliage on the banks shut out the camps and stores and dire confusion of "the Hook," we gently glided into the quiet reaches of the canal, the broad, rock-strewn river shimmering in the sun on the right (or "starboard side," as the boys commenced to call it), bordered on the west by the mighty spurs of the Blue Ridge, with not a sound to break the stillness, it was as if they had left the riotous tumult of war for some lonely land of rest.

In truth, there could be no greater contrast to the awful storms of battle from which we had just emerged at Gettysburg. The scream of shells and the thunderous roar of artillery were replaced by the soft notes of birds twittering in the trees, whose branches swayed in the water, or the distant caw of a solitary crow circling over the quiet river.

It was hard to realize, as the Battery floated down, out of sight or sound of the exciting life of which it had been part and parcel for two years, shut in from the world by a green wall of verdure on either bank, that only a few days before it was battling for life amid a quarter of a million of armed soldiers.

That the boys enjoyed this unwonted break in their soldier life was very apparent. Stretched on the deck through the long summer day, some smoking, some discussing the recent battle, others sleeping, or lazily observing the scenery, it was an Elysian dream to the weary marches, the rough handling, the desperate fighting to which the Battery had become inured.

Then the "foraging" was something to delight a veteran's heart. It was so easy to leap from the boats onto the bank, scurry up the hills to a farm house and return loaded with milk, butter, eggs, fruit, etc., and that without having to watch every bush and tree, as in the old days in Virginia, for a possible sharpshooter, eager to send his leaden compliments from the end of a rifle.

But this pleasant kind of soldiering could n't last long, and about noon of the third day out the boats pulled into Georgetown, where I met them.

The Battery was disembarked and marched through Washington to Camp Barry, northeast of the city. This was supposed to be a recruiting camp, but during our stay here it was a camp of misery and degradation. A Lieutenant-Colonel Monroe, of Rhode Island, was in command, whom I learned to heartily despise. He proved to be a martinet of the meanest kind; we had trouble; I made application to be ordered to the front; it was returned, *disapproved*, with the endorsement, "This officer desires to evade duty, etc."

It appeared odd to me, that asking to be sent to the field should be construed as a "desire to evade duty." However, I made another application. This time I appealed to General Hunt, Chief of Artillery of the Army of the Potomac. My application passed through General Meade's headquarters, and was referred to General Halleck, who caused an order to be issued at once, directing me to report, etc., without delay. In this manner I defeated an attempt to convert our heroes of Gettysburg into laborers, for the purpose of keeping up this "pet" camp by sweeping and digging in the hot sun from morning until night. (Monroe was sent to the field as Chief of Artillery, Fifth Corps; his record was not brilliant, as might be supposed.)

One glorious August morning at 5 A. M. we left Camp Barry, without a pang of regret, marching to Alexandria, Va., where I was to wait for an escort.

The army was stationed near Warrenton, Va., at this time and Mosby had been troublesome on the roads leading from Washington into Virginia. I did not believe he would molest us, therefore, with an escort of six (a sergeant and five enlisted men of the cavalry), I decided to move forward. Four of my escort were sent to the front and two to the rear; two of those in front were instructed to ride well out on side roads and remain on guard until the Battery passed, when they were to rejoin their comrades in front. The guns were so disposed that the front, flanks and rear were well protected; a surprise was out of the question.

At Alexandria I had found a train of sutlers anxious to get to the army. They were determined to follow the Battery. I plainly explained to them my intention to prevent Mosby from capturing their train, if possible, and told them that if the enemy got among their wagons I would use canister without regard to sutlers.

"Now," said I, "if you care to take the chances, all right."

They took the chances, and I had a train fully half a mile long as far as Centerville. We were not interfered with, and reached the army in due time, and were assigned to the artillery reserve.

After the march over the Rapidan in pursuit of Lee's army, (which we found), we quietly slipped back into camp near Warrenton, and remained there until the Battery was disbanded by order of the Secretary of War. Previous to this it had been reduced from six to four guns by reason of its decimated ranks.

While in camp here the spirit of discontent, always prevalent while in winter quarters, again manifested itself. Those enlisted men who believed they were unjustly held in service, again took advantage of the situation to agitate the question of their discharge.

The discussion of this matter first began in 1861, while we were camped in Lower Maryland. I at that time made an application to have the Battery sent to its regiment, the First Engineers, New York Volunteers. The facts were plainly set forth, as a true copy herewith will attest. I had no desire to have the men retained as artillerists against their will, knowing the matter would give more or less cause for dissension. But my papers were returned disapproved and the claim disregarded by reason of the exigencies of the service. The following is a true copy, with endorsements, etc.:

"CAMP HOOKER, LOWER POTOMAC, MD.
"*28th January, 1862.*

"*Brig. Gen'l Joseph Hooker,*
"*Commanding Division.*

Sir:—The Battery under my command was organganized 4th September, 1861, as Company 'L' of Col. Serrell's Volunteer Engineer Regiment, to do duty as a Battery of Light Artillery, and was mustered into the United Service as such, and a large majority of the men composing it were enlisted under the impression, founded on representations in good faith made to them at the time, that the Battery would be attached to the said regiment, and that they would receive engineers' pay, viz.: $17 per month. We left New York 25th October, by order of Col. Serrell, and arrived in Washington 26th October. On the 27th, reported to General Barry and made application to be equipped as a battery of light artillery, and to be attached to the above regiment, as originally contemplated. General Barry then informed me that he could not equip us as a battery attached to said regiment, inasmuch as all batteries hitherto attached to regiments of infantry had been or would be detached therefrom, under orders from headquarters, at the same time expressing his readiness to equip us as an independent battery of light artillery, in which case the men would receive the ordinary pay of artillerists, viz.: $13 per month. He further led me to suppose that it was a matter of much doubt whether any portion of the regiment would receive more than the pay of second class engineers, and stated that our being organized and equipped at that time as an independent battery would not militate against our being attached as a battery to the regiment at some future time, should our application therefor meet with the approval of the proper authorities. At the suggestion of General Barry I communicated these facts to the men of my command, and all except thirteen expressed their willingness, under the circumstances, to serve as an independent battery. I then reported to General Barry, and asked that we be so equipped. On 2d and 4th November we received our battery, and have done duty as light artillery since that time. On 25th November we left Washington under orders from Headquarters, Army of the Potomac, and arrived here and reported 27th November. Since our arrival here it has been ascertained from letters from members of the Volunteer Engineer Regiment that they had been paid off at the rate of $17 a month, the pay of first-class engineers, and Colonel Serrell has given us to understand that he has been assured that, if we could be attached to his command, the men would receive pay at the same rate, as they were told at the time of their enlistment.

"Under all the circumstances of the case, therefore, of which the above is a brief, impartial statement, we deem it eminently proper respectfully to make application that we be attached to the said regiment as a battery of light artillery, as originally contemplated, and that the non-commissioned officers and privates of this command be declared to be entitled to pay at the rate fixed by law for the payment of engineers.

"The above statement is made at the request of the non-commissioned officers and privates of my command and respectfully submitted for your consideration.

"I am, General, your most obedient servant,
"(Signed) J. E. SMITH,
"*Capt. Comm'd'g 4th N. Y. Battery.*"

"(Endorsement.)

"Respectfully submitted with the request that it may receive the immediate attention of the Major-General Commanding.

"JOSEPH HOOKER,
"*Brig.-Gen. Comm'd'g.*

"HEADQUARTERS OF THE ARMY OF THE POTOMAC,
"*January 29, 1862.*

"Respectfully returned to Brigadier-General Barry, Chief of Artillery.

"By command of MAJOR-GENERAL MCCLELLAN.
"JAMES A. HARDIE,
"*Lt. Col. A. D. C.*"

"(Endorsement.)

"Respectfully returned. This battery is now attached to Hooker's Division, and I have no other battery available, at present, to take its place. It can not be spared from its present duties. Captain Smith is somewhat in error in one of his statements. I never informed him that his battery might eventually be attached to Serrell's Regt., but on the contrary told him most positively that it was against the orders of Major-General McClellan for batteries to be attached to Regt's of foot, and I doubtless told him, as I have many others under similar circumstances, that if Serrell's Regt. belonged to the Army of the Potomac, the Battery might possibly be assigned to the same Division. I furthermore directed Captain Smith to inform his men that their pay would be that of light artillery soldiers — no more. If it is decided to send this company to its regiment (which is now at Port Royal) I would respectfully recommend that the guns, horses, and all other light art'y. equipment be left with this army, where they are much needed.

"(Signed)   WILLIAM F. BARRY,
Brig. Gen., Chief of Art'y.

Jan. 30, '62.

The matter came up again in the early spring of '62, and Major Wainwright, Division Chief of Artillery, was authorized by General Hooker to investigate the matter. The cause of this second trouble was owing to a few persistent enlisted men who made false representations of the affair to the General, not flattering to myself; but I had done all in my power to have the men sent to the regiment. By following the instructions of Colonel Serrell, I had gotten into difficulty, — whereas, if I had quietly remained in New York and allowed myself to be commissioned as Major, no blame could rest upon me. After sacrificing my personal interests for what I believed to be the best interests of the company, I now felt conscious of my error; and, as before stated, had no wish to prevent the men from being transferred, even if I had the power, which I had not.

The result of the second, or Wainwright, investigation was not imparted to me. I only know that no further action was taken; there was no further trouble on this score until May and June, 1863, when Captain Randolph, Chief of Corps Artillery, was directed by General Sickles to look into the matter, presumably in response to a communication from the men.

This also ended in smoke. But in the early winter of

1863 some men deserted, and, returning to New York City, were discharged by order of the Supreme Court of the State on the ground of false enlistment. This, of course, was liable to have a demoralizing effect on the Battery, so I then applied to have the balance of the men, who were enlisted under the same conditions or promise, transferred to the regiment or discharged the service.

The matter was referred to the Secretary of War, who ordered that those men who enlisted, etc., be transferred to the regiment, and the balance of the company transferred to the batteries from the State to serve the balance of their term of enlistment. Those officers who did not wish to go to the regiment were mustered out of service.

And so ended the career of the 4th New York Independent Battery, after a service of two years, three months and nineteen days, having been disbanded December 23, 1863.

"Ne'er shall its glory fade."

Many of the men who served the balance of their term of service in other batteries distinguished themselves and reflected honor on the old Battery by their bravery and ability, some of them returning home with a captain's commission. One of these was John B. Johnston, mentioned in the early part of this history as having been wounded at Williamsburg.

While on this subject I am reminded that a certain enlisted man, one Thomas Graham, who was discharged in December, 1861, on certificate of disability, volunteered this remarkable piece of information to the G.

A. R. Post to which he had made application for membership:

"I enlisted in Company "L," 1st Regiment Engineers, New York Volunteers, but the company was surreptitiously run away from New York by Capt. J. E. Smith and forced to serve as a battery."

I hope Graham has made a better record as a member of the G. A. R. than he did as a soldier for the short period that he wore "Uncle Sam's" uniform.

In regard to the officers of the Battery, I am responsible for the first four Lieutenants. Great pains were taken to make proper selections, but mistakes will occur.

Joseph E. Nairn, First Lieutenant, Sr., served three months in Varian's Battery, and by his soldierly bearing then attracted my attention. While he was connected with the 4th New York Battery his conduct fully sustained the high estimate I had placed upon his qualifications and character.

Charles H. Scott, First Lieutenant, Jr., served as a commissioned officer in one of the Connecticut regiments in Tyler's Brigade in the three months' service. I thought he had some experience which would be serviceable.

William T. McLean, Second Lieutenant, Jr., also served three months in Varian's Battery.

J. Courtland Parker, Second Lieutenant, Jr., was a young lawyer of great promise. His early taking off cut short a career which had given evidence of much usefulness.

APPENDIX.

Extract from Volume 1, Report of Adjutant-General of the State of New York, 1868 (page 169).

FIRST TROOP WASHINGTON GRAYS.

"HEADQUARTERS
"SQUADRON WASHINGTON GRAYS, N. G. S. N. Y.
"NEW YORK, *December 24, 1867.*

"The following is a brief sketch of the services rendered to the U. S. Government, during the late war, by the above company:

"In April, 1861, being then attached to the 8th Regiment, N. Y. S. Militia, and known and designated as company "I," they were, with that regiment, the first to respond to the call of the President for 75,000 men, for the term of three months, to aid in the suppression of the rebellion. They accordingly enlisted in the United States service on the 18th day of April, 1861, as an artillery corps, under the command of Captain Joshua M. Varian, now Brigadier-General of the Third Brigade, N. G., to serve the aforementioned term of three months, and to be disposed of during the term of their enlistment as was thought proper by their superior officers. They left New York on the morning of the 19th, on the steamer *Montgomery*, under sealed orders, which were not made known till the steamer was well out to sea. This was the first knowledge the troop had of their destination, which was Annapolis, Md., and at which place they arrived on the 22d, and were rejoined by the infantry of the 8th Regiment, N. Y. S. M., under command of Col. Lyons. The company had been detached from the regiment on leaving New York, as one vessel was not sufficiently large to accommodate the whole command. After being quartered with the regiment a few days, they were again separated by the infantry being ordered on to Washington, while the troop remaining at Annapolis, performed guard duty on the Annapolis river and Chesapeake Bay with the 13th Regment, N. Y. S. M., under command of Col. Smith.

The post at that time was under command of General Benjamin F. Butler. A few days after the departure of the regiment from Annapolis, two detachments of the company with one company of the 13th Regiment, by orders of General Butler, embarked on the steam tug *Stevens* for the purpose of regaining the light ship formerly stationed at Smith's Point, on the Chesapeake Bay, which had been taken by the rebels and placed in a position in a small creek running in from the bay — their object being to mislead vessels in the night. The vessel was found about two miles from the entrance of Smith Creek, with no one on board to dispute the right of possession, and not until lines had been made fast and the vessel had begun to move out of the creek, did the rebels open fire on the *Stevens* from the shores each side, where they had been laying in ambush; four or five volleys from the infantry, together with three or four rounds of canister completely routed them. They proved to be two companies of 1st South Carolina regiment; their loss was two killed, a lieutenant and private; seven wounded and thirteen prisoners. Three days from that time, the troops were ordered to rejoin the 8th Regiment at Arlington Heights, to strengthen the forces about the Capitol at Washington. It was with the regiment ten days, when it was again separated by being ordered to join a Connecticut Brigade, and proceed to the village of Falls Church, the farthest outpost from

Washington, where it did very effective service on the roads leading from Falls Church to Vienna and Fairfax Court-House, capturing a number of rebel scouts and spies; also in obtaining a great amount of valuable information. In the grand advance, which commenced on the 14th of July, this troop, with a battery of six-pound brass field pieces, had the right of the line of the middle division, commanded by Gen. E. D. Keyes and General Tyler, and, at Fairfax Court-House, fired the first ball that opened the campaign in northeastern Virginia, driving the rebels in the wildest confusion. The troop continued in the advance of the division through Fairfax Court-House, thence to Germantown, and so on to Centreville, meeting with very little opposition. After leaving the Court-House, they were then relieved by Ayer's U. S. Battery, after having been in the advance four days, from the 14th to the 18th of July; was then held in reserve during the battle of Centreville. On the 18th, were preparing to go into action, when our forces were called off by General McDowell, commanding Department of Virginia. Its time expired on the 17th, and on the 20th it returned to Washington, and from thence to New York, where it was mustered out of service by reason of expiration of term of enlistment.

Immediately after being mustered out, Lieut. J. E. Smith, with about forty members of the troop, formed the nucleus of the famous 4th New York Independent Battery, which served during the war with as bright a record as any in the whole army. What was left then of the troop was reorganized under Captain Robert Brown, and was again in service during the invasion of Pennsylvania by the rebels, in June, 1863. It was engaged both as cavalry and artillery, at Carlisle, Shippensburg, Scotland, Chambersburgh, Oyster Point and Kingston. Was recalled to New York before the expiration of its time, on account of the riots then taking place; although enlisted for but thirty, it served forty-six days, and was again mustered out of service. The command was, in 1861, composed of 125 men, besides its officers. After its first muster out, it is safe to say two-thirds of its members re-enlisted, mostly under their former Lieutenant, James E. Smith, but many of them in other regiments. Out of nine that joined the 7th N. J. V., six were killed; about thirty were killed and wounded in the 4th Independent Battery.

MAJ. S. M. SWIFT,
Commanding.

JAMES TANNER.

THE CAREER

OF

CORPORAL TANNER

CHIVALRY in its best sense did not perish when the steel-clad knights and men-at-arms passed away with the advent of powder and rifled guns. The daring deeds and wild adventures of the mailed heroes of mediæval romance pale their ineffectual fires before the cool courage, the sublime devotion that carried the defenders of the American Republic into the jaws of death as unshrinkingly as ever the Cid or great Godfrey de Bouillon rode into battle.

Among the gallant array whose names have won deathless renown on the sanguinary fields of our great Civil War none is more widely esteemed, or is more deserving of his fame, than that hero of the rank and file known of all men as "Corporal Tanner."

But of his career from the farm to the ranks, "through the valley of the shadow of death," to honorable service in his native State and then to the high and responsible position of Commissioner of Pensions of the United States, of all these bare facts only are generally known. A brief sketch of his life—never before published—may be of interest to the American people. It is needless to say that it will be welcomed by the million and more ex-soldiers whose cause is the dearest thing on earth to his brave heart, and to whose service he has given twenty-five years of unselfish devotion by word and pen and deed.

JAMES TANNER was born near Richmondville, Schoharie Co., New York, April 4, 1844. His early life was spent on the farm, working in the fields in summer, and attending the district school in winter, besides "doing the chores" about the farm which fall to the lot of every country boy. That he profited above the average by the meagre facilities afforded him for an education is evident from the fact that before reaching his eighteenth year he was engaged in teaching school himself.

At the outbreak of the war, although still a mere boy, fired with the patriotic ardor that was his by birthright, he enlisted in Company "C," 87th New York Volunteer Infantry, and went with his regiment to the front. The 87th was assigned to Kearny's Division, and with it took part in the Peninsular campaign, being engaged in the battles of Williamsburg, Fair Oaks, Siege of Yorktown, Seven Days' Battles before Richmond, and Malvern Hill. Mr. Tanner, in one of his lectures, gave a modest but vivid account of some incidents of his soldier life. As it is quite brief, it is here reproduced.

"When the war broke out I was just seventeen years old. I was a big, green country boy, and had never seen a railroad train until I went away to enlist. My good old father had brought me up to glory in my native land, and he believed that its liberties should be preserved at any cost. But he was, as far as I was concerned, like Deacon Stubbs of Maine and the prohibition law. He was 'in favor of the law but agin its enforcement.' My father wanted the country saved, but, like many others, he did n't want *his* boy to go to war. We had many discussions on the subject, and one hot afternoon, when we were out in the field, I told him that my mind was made up, I was going to enlist. So one day when it was raining so hard that you would expect that no one in his senses would stir out of doors, I slipped away to town and was duly mustered in. When I found myself in the blue I wrote to father that I would get a few days' leave of absence if he would promise not to detain me when I came home. He readily acquiesced, and so I had the consolation of going to the front with his consent and blessing.

"My first experience of what was in store for us was when we arrived at Fortress Monroe. It was late in the afternoon and we camped in a field. When night came on I selected a nice, dry furrow (which reminded me of home) for my bed, and wrapping my blanket around me, with my knapsack for a pillow, I was soon sound asleep. It was the first time I had ever slept out without a roof of some kind to cover me. Along about midnight I was awakened by a roaring noise and started up in terror, but it was only an old-fashioned Virginia rainstorm sweeping over us, and as I lay in a furrow I had the full benefit of the torrents of water that poured down it."

Speaking of Malvern Hill and the Seven Days' Fight, Mr. Tanner relates this little personal incident, which will be appreciated by the boys who were at the front:

"We were stationed in a field filled with blackberry bushes, and it did n't take us long to find out that the berries were ripe and plentiful. I stood my gun against a tree and proceeded to fill up an ever-aching void (in those days) in my interior. The shells were flying pretty thick over us and I came to the conclusion that we would soon have a warm time of it. I had just secured a great big berry and was about to put it in my mouth when a shell hit the tree where my gun was standing and a shower of branches and bark struck me. I thought the top of my head was gone, but felt very much relieved when I found that I had nothing worse to show for this close call than an enormously swelled lip. But I lost the blackberry."

Subsequently, the 87th participated in the battles of Warrenton, Bristow Station and Manassas. The subject of this sketch was with his regiment through it all, serving as a corporal, and his gallantry and efficiency gave promise of a brilliant career, when the chances of battle put a sudden and terrible end to the ambitious boy's dreams of military glory in the service of his country.

At the Second Battle of Bull Run, August 30, 1862, Robinson's Brigade, of which the 87th was part, held the extreme right of our line, in front of Stonewall Jackson's Corps. About 3 P. M. of that fateful day the enemy's artillery had gotten the exact range of this line and opened on it with a terrific storm of shot and shell which nothing mortal could withstand. As the only means of saving them the men were ordered to lie close to the ground until a lull in the murderous fire to which they were exposed might offer opportunity to use their guns. While thus hugging the earth, his face to the foe, his musket at a ready, a hurtling fragment from a bursting shell struck the brave young corporal's left lower leg, nearly severing the foot at the ankle, and then shattering the right leg below the knee into a mass of crushed flesh and splintered bone. At the first chance he was gently carried from the front by his comrades, unconscious and apparently dying, and placed in the field hospital where the surgeons at once amputated both legs about four inches below the knee.

Meanwhile the Union line had been broken and his comrades were forced to leave him at a farm house with other desperately wounded soldiers. The enemy soon had the house within their lines and made him and his companions in suffering prisoners. Some ten days afterwards they were all paroled and taken to Fairfax Seminary Hospital near Alexandria. Mr. Tanner's personal recollection of that momentous event in his career is thus succinctly given in a private letter to a friend which was published in the *National Tribune* in 1887:

"Two or three nights prior to my being wounded at the second Bull Run, my regiment (the 87th N. Y.) was stationed along the Orange & Alexandria Railroad at Manassas, Bristow, Catlett's and the bridge near Catlett's. Jackson struck in there (at Manassas) and tore us pretty well to pieces. John C. Robinson, then our Brigadier, issued an order that the enlisted men of the 87th should report to and maneuver with the 105th Pa., and so at the time I was wounded we were under command of Colonel Craige, of that regiment. Just prior to my being struck, General Robinson had ordered us to fix bayonets and lie down, and as we did so I threw one heel up over the other and was in that position when hit. I had been talking with the sergeant-major of the 105th Pennsylvania, and knew his position from the chevrons on his sleeves, but was ignorant of his name. The first intimation I had of the extent of my injury was when he jumped to his feet and exclaimed: 'My God! look at that poor boy with both feet gone!'

"When the boys picked me up they laid me on a blanket — no stretcher being available — and twisted a musket in on each side and lifted me to their shoulders. Neither of my legs had been entirely severed; my feet were hanging by shreds of flesh. The blanket was short, and lying on it on my face, I looked under and saw my feet dangling by the skin as they hung off of the other end. Some kind-hearted soul gently lifted them and laid them on the edge of the blanket."

The sergeant-major of whom Mr. Tanner speaks is now (or was recently) a farmer residing near Washington, Kansas. He wrote a long letter to the Corporal under date of May 5, 1887, which has also been published, and extracts from which are here given:

"When Colonel Craige ordered me to take charge of your squad you seemed to be the only one to whom they looked for commands (there were, I think, seventeen of you), and I remember that you impressed me as being a young man of more than ordinary intelligence and ability; and I left control of the boys almost entirely in your hands, and that is how we happened to be together when you were struck. I know that your squad had been assigned to our regiment and that we were in line of battle when you were hit by a cannon-ball. I am led to believe it was a cannon-ball because there was no after-explosion. I recollect that it was the whirr of the missile that caused me to look up when I saw it coming for us. I remember well the house above us and a little to our right, with an old orchard, mostly peach, between. We lay in a hollow where a tree had once stood, you on your left and I on my right side as we talked. While talking we noticed a 'speller' near a peach tree just above us. I crawled up to it and as I laid my hand on it I heard, and then looking up, saw the whizzing fragment coming down for us. My nose went into the ground till I heard the thud behind me, when I looked and saw at once your sad fate; the bleeding, feetless legs sticking up so shocked me that I have no recollection of what I may have said. I will quote verbatim from my journal, written the next day while we lay near Centreville:

"'A few of the 87th New York boys were with us, and one of them, lying within five or six feet of me, had both feet cut off by a cannon ball that struck him. He seemed to be a brave lad, but it was a heartrending sight to see his look as he stuck up to view his footless legs. I have witnessed many horrid scenes, but never one that sent such a thrill of painful feeling through me as this. * * *

"Fraternally yours,
"R. J. BOVINGTON,
"*Sergeant Major 105th Pa., and*
"*1st Lieut. Co. 'I' 105th Pa.*"

Capt. B. F. Butterfield, of Erie, Pa., contributes his quota to this "o'er-true tale." He was the soldier who tenderly lifted up the Corporal's mangled feet and replaced them on the blanket. He writes:

"I was then (August 30, 1862,) a private of Co. 'B,' 63d Pa. Our Brigade, as far as my memory now serves me, consisted of the 57th, 63d, and 105th Pa., 87th N. Y., and the 20th Ind., Gen. Robinson commanding.

"There was a sort of shallow ravine or dip about the center of the field in which we lay, which ran at right angles to the front. The bed of a small, dry rivulet ran through this. The rebels seemed to have discovered us early. I think it was from the men on the hill picking peaches, the trees of which were full and ripe. I remember there were yells from our line of 'Get down!' 'Come down out of that!' to the fellows on the hill. It was but a few moments until a battery of at least four guns was pitching shells at and over us in a lively manner. The 105th, I think, was the next regiment to us, and it was immediately after the explosion of a shell in the air rather close to us that you were carried by in a blanket. I thought at first that you were a 105th man, but seeing your 'New York jacket,' concluded that you belonged to Hobart Ward's (Second) Brigade.

"Your face was that of a youth of about eighteen, and as our boys came up, with expressions of pity on their faces, you remarked, if you recollect it, 'Never mind, boys,' or something like that. I thought it very plucky at the time, and the incident left a vivid impression on my memory, and although the day previous and on many battle-fields, both before and after, I witnessed death and wounds in many forms, the circumstances of this case I shall always distinctly recall."

Mr. Isaac W. Lawrence, at present an official in the Department of Taxes and Assessments of the city of Brooklyn, was one of the soldiers who carried Corporal Tanner off the field when wounded. His recollection of the incident is very clear and minute, and he thus related it to a reporter of the New York *Herald* soon after Mr. Tanner's appointment as Commissioner of Pensions:

"James Tanner was a tall but boyish-looking soldier when the enemy's fire cut him down. He was color corporal of Company 'C,' 87th New York Volunteers. I was a private in 'H' Company of the same regiment. We were attached to the First Brigade, First Division, Third Corps. General John C. Robinson was our Brigade Commander when we came up from the Peninsula and joined Pope's Army. Kearny's Division was sent ahead, while our Brigade went along the line of the Manassas road, from Warrenton to Manassas Junction by way of Sulphur Springs. Five companies were held at Catlett's Station while the other five companies of our regiment were sent to Manassas.

"This was in the latter part of the summer of 1862 when Stonewall Jackson got in the rear of the army. Three days before the second battle of Bull Run, and the day before the fight at Bristow Station, Jackson swooped down and gobbled our five companies at Manassas Junction.

"The next day Hooker and Kearny engaged Jackson at Bristow. There were two fights there. After being cut up so, the 87th was consolidated with, or attached to, the 105th Pennsylvania. We had no field officers left and only two or three captains when we formed the left wing of the Pennsylvania regiment.

"From Bristow we marched to the battle-field of Bull Run. Most of the remnant of our regiment got scattered. We moved along with the Pennsylvania boys to the right of the line, where on a knoll we supported a battery.

"We were subjected to a sharp fire of shell and shrapnel from the guns of Hill's Corps. The 'rebs' were trying to turn the flank of our army. We were ordered to lie close and get ready to receive them.

"A shell burst over our heads. I was lying alongside of Corporal Tanner. The butt end of the shell came down, struck Tanner's left ankle, and passing through that member, lodged in his right ankle, severing the left and shattering the right. Both feet hung by shreds of flesh. We had to pick the metal out of the right leg. 'Good Lord! Look at that boy. He has both legs off!' exclaimed the sergeant-major of the 105th Pennsylvania.

"'Yes,' answered the plucky Corporal, 'and if you don't get me out of here pretty quick my head will be off.'

"'Take him right back to the surgeon, boys,' said an officer.

"Then Sergeant Sproul, a corporal and myself placed Tanner on a blanket and carried him to the rear, where we got a stretcher for him. A surgeon amputated both legs.

"Then the fire of the enemy came nearer and nearer to where we were, and taking him on the stretcher, we carried him about half a mile to a house which was used as an hospital. But it was full of wounded, and we laid him down on the ground beside the door.

"The Johnnies were hotly pressing our lines and Tanner said: 'Boys, never mind me. Get back for your own safety. Give me a canteen of water and leave me.'

"I filled a canteen from a well near by and gave it to him. Then we boys scattered in every direction.

"When I came back from the army on furlough in March, 1864, I was going down Broadway one day, and was in the neighborhood of Trinity Church when I saw a young man walking towards me with a peculiar gait, and carrying a cane.

"'Hello! Company 'H'!' cried the young man.

"'Hello yourself, but you've got the best of me,' said I.

"'What! Don't you remember Jim Tanner?'

"'You ain't Jim Tanner. He had both legs cut off; you haven't.'

"'Feel them,' said the Corporal, for such he really was.

"I felt and saw they were artificial. Of course our meeting was a pleasant one.

"When Mr. Tanner was made Collector of Taxes for Brooklyn he sent for me and appointed me to a clerkship in his office, and I have been here ever since."

Mr. William A. Shute, now an employé of the Pension Bureau, was a fellow-sufferer with Corporal Tanner on this occasion, having lost a leg at the same battle. His experience will be read with interest. He writes thus under date of May 1, 1892:

"*Dear Captain Smith:* My recollection of the disastrous Second Bull Run is naturally pretty clear, for I ended my army service on that bloody field.

"During the battle a field hospital was established in a farm yard just to the rear of where Rickett's Division had made their splendid charge. Surgeon J. S. Jamieson, of the 86th New York, was in charge, assisted by a nephew of Gov. Curtin, a surgeon in some Pennsylvania regiment. We were, of course, inside the enemy's lines and prisoners of war. Here were grouped together 215 of the desperately wounded, and among them six of us who had lost seven legs, Corporal Tanner contributing the double amputation. The first night we passed there with the dark canopy of a stormy sky for a covering, which eventually dissolved and poured down on us a drenching rain. Though this was disagreeable enough to us poor, helpless fellows, yet I have often thought since that it may have been a blessing in disguise by the unstinted application of cold water it afforded to our fevered limbs. After a couple of days the Van Pelt residence was taken and used as a hospital and we legless victims of war were carried in and laid in rows in the hall. The owner of the house came along in the afternoon and his wrath at seeing his residence used for such purposes was extreme, but little attention was paid to his bluster.

"Late in the evening of September 2d, Medical Director T. H. Wingfield, Inspector and Paroling Officer of the C. S. A., came around and paroled the wounded, but sent some ten comrades who had been caring for us off to Richmond. There was only one sound man left with us, a bright, obliging young fellow who had been acting as hospital steward for our surgeons, and who certainly had his hands full in responding to the numerous demands made upon him. This youth is now known as the Hon. Charles E. Coon, who was a few years ago Assistant Secretary of the United States Treasury.

"That night a large tent was put up in the yard, and the worst cases, among whom were Corporal Tanner and myself, were removed to it. There we stayed ten days and nights, suffering both for food and care. The first four days, especially, we came pretty near being starved. I remember that I traded my covered canteen with one of the Confederate guards for his battered old apology for one and two hard tack to boot. Then we received some supplies under a flag of truce, but had to divide with 'our friends, the enemy.'

"The weather was excessively warm, and with no one to attend to us except the embryo Treasury official alluded to, it is no wonder that we all suffered dreadfully, and some died whose lives might have been saved under other surroundings.

"I lay next to Tanner and, although he was but a boy of eighteen, I never saw a wounded soldier bear his misfortune with more nerve and patience. Weak and exhausted as I was, he was still more helpless, and I am glad to know that I was able, in a wavering kind of a way, to be of some service to the gallant boy whose fortitude I admired.

"On the 9th of September, just as the sun was sinking behind the Bull Run Mountains, the last train of ambulances bore us away from the famous battle-field with its immortal memories, and though we had a long and wearisome ride through the night, its miseries were wonderfully relieved by the thought that it was towards our 'ain counteree' that we were going. We reached Fairfax Seminary at 10 A. M. the succeeding day, glad to be able to rest our weary bodies on something softer than the bare ground of Bull Run battle-field, and after that we had every attention that medical skill could supply. Very truly yours,

"W. A. SHUTE,
"*Late of Co. 'I,' 13th Mass. Vol. Inf.*"

In Fairfax Hospital was continued his long struggle for life, with the odds terribly against him, but a vigorous constitution and a stern determination to live brought him through this dreadful time when he tasted the bitterness of death daily. His courage never faltered, and when he began to improve his first thought was: "What can I do, thus crippled, to hold my place among men?" His ambition could not brook the thought that he must be contented to go to the wall in the world's battle because of his misfortune.

After a long course of treatment in the hospital he became strong enough to be removed to the old home in Schoharie, where his native air and the cordial sympathy of every man, woman and child in the county did wonders in bringing back his health. He was skillfully fitted with artificial limbs, which he soon learned to manage passably well. Through the influence of his friends, who admired his plucky fight against adverse circumstances, he was appointed Deputy Doorkeeper of the Assembly, at Albany, and subsequently held various positions under the Legislature, which he filled with credit. His misfortune, his nerve and his undoubted abilities soon made his name known beyond his native State, and in 1864 he came to Washington to take a clerkship in the War Department under Secretary Stanton.

On the night of the assassination of President Lincoln he was called upon to take notes of the first official evidence regarding the tragedy, and this duty brought him the sad privilege of standing by the bedside of the dying President.

The monotonous routine of clerical life, however,

soon wearied his energetic spirit, and in December, 1865, he resigned his position, returned to Richmondville and began the study of law with Judge William C. Lamont. He married in the same year a daughter of Alfred C. White, of Jefferson, N. Y.

He was admitted to the bar in 1869. He then accepted a position in the New York Custom House and took up his residence in Brooklyn, where his eloquence, his vim and tact soon made him a man of mark in the councils of his party. On a competitive examination he rose to the position of Deputy Collector and served as such four years under Gen. Chester A. Arthur.

In 1871 he was the Republican candidate for the Assembly from the Fourth, King's County, district, but was counted out in the election frauds of that year. He was nominated for County Register by the Republicans in 1876, and while the Democratic ticket had a majority of 19,000, he was defeated by less than 2,000 votes, a magnificent tribute to his popularity among all classes of his fellow-citizens.

Connected as he had been with the Grand Army of the Republic almost from its inception, no man more enjoyed the esteem and confidence of his comrades than "Corporal Tanner." They knew him to possess sound judgment, ripe experience and enthusiastic devotion to the Order, so it was but natural that he should eventually become a leader. In 1876 he was elected Commander of the Department of New York. He assumed the office at a time when discouragement and disappointment pervaded the organization, growing out of the neglect of the State to provide for her helpless and homeless disabled veterans.

The soldiers, stung by the ingratitude of those in whose defense they had braved death and sacrificed their health, began to despair. The outlook was discouraging, indeed. But Commander Tanner threw himself into the work, heart and soul. Calling to his assistance that true patriot, Rev. Henry Ward Beecher, the good work was inaugurated by a mass meeting in Brooklyn, when $13,000 was subscribed towards a Home for the veterans. During the two years that Mr. Tanner was Department Commander—for he served two terms—he traversed the State from the sea to the lakes, setting forth in glowing words the veterans' needs, the debt of gratitude due them from the State, and the shame of degrading her maimed defenders to the condition of alms-house paupers. He so fired the hearts of the citizens that a flood of petitions poured in on the legislature, and tardy justice was meted out. A magnificent "Soldiers' Home" was erected at Bath, Steuben County, where six hundred disabled veterans find the repose and comforts of a home. Truly "a monument more durable than brass" to Commander Tanner's zeal and energy in behalf of his comrades.

Mr. Tanner has been conspicuous for years in securing just and generous pension legislation from Congress. He has been a familiar figure before the Committees of the Senate and House having these matters in charge, and his eloquent pleas have had a powerful effect in shaping legislative action for the benefit of those who had suffered in defense of their country. He gave his time, his labor and his talents to this cause without fee or reward, paying his own expenses on his frequent trips to the Capital in behalf of his disabled comrades.

To show the broad-minded liberality of Mr. Tanner, an incident, or rather, action, may be here related, although it occurred subsequent to the period of which we are speaking. Although a man of most positive views, with the courage of his convictions in all places and circumstances, a life-long sufferer from wounds received in the war, yet has he been quick to lend his help to the sufferers who fought on the other side, "not," as he said, "on account of their cause, but for the reason that they were brave Americans." While on a visit to Richmond, Va., the sad condition of numerous maimed and helpless soldiers of the Confederacy was on one occasion the subject of discussion among several ex-members of both armies, and their pitiful lot was contrasted with that of the Union soldiers, for whom the Government could not do too much. Corporal Tanner's heart was touched, and his active brain worked up a scheme for their relief. He suggested that the citizens of Virginia should take the matter in hand, build and equip a home, and then demand that the State should care for it. The idea took at once, and acting upon his advice appeals were made to the soldiers of the Grand Army for aid. Further, a great meeting was held, under his inspiration, at the Academy of Music in Brooklyn, to aid in this object, which was addressed, among others, by Rev. Henry Ward Beecher and Rev. J. M. Foster, at which some $1,600 was realized for the proposed Confederate Home. This was the nucleus of a fund which has since swelled to $25,000. So grateful were the Southern friends of the institution that when the work was inaugurated at Richmond this stalwart Republican was unanimously selected as one of the Trustees of the Home, which position, however, he declined to accept, although assuring the promoters that it would always be a profound satisfaction to him to feel that he had been able to do something towards providing the comforts of life for some of the crippled, homeless veterans who had gone down with the cause for which they had battled in vain.

In November, 1877, Mr. Tanner was appointed Collector of Taxes for the City of Brooklyn, which office he held with universal acceptance for eight years, through both the Republican and Democratic municipal administrations.

With that restless energy characteristic of the man, he instituted numerous reforms in the system of conducting the business, extending greater facilities to the tax-payers and reducing the expenses of the office fully fifty per cent.

To show the estimation in which he was held by his fellow citizens a few extracts from the leading journals of the city are quoted.

The Brooklyn *Daily Times* of November 30, 1885, calls his administration "A Phenomenal Success," and then goes on to say.

"When he entered the office some ten years ago, the receipt of $400,000 was considered a big thing for the first day on which taxes could be received. Since he introduced the system of payment by check through the mails, the payments have so increased that a vast amount of money is thrown into the municipal treasury the moment the civic authorities can legally receive it. Last year the amount in the hands of the Tax Collector, paid by check, on the 1st of December, was $2,000,000. The year before it was $1,500,000. To-day Collector Tanner is of the opinion that by tomorrow morning he will have in his possession $3,000,000 of the taxes of 1886, or not far from half of the entire levy. The Collector and his cash room work until midnight every night."

The Brooklyn *Daily Eagle* of December 2, 1885, says:

"Collector Tanner paid to the Treasurer last evening, as the first day's receipts for the taxes of 1885, $3,236,885.69, as against $2,762,306 on the first day of payment last year. He was enabled to make this large payment through the system of furnishing bills and allowing property owners to send checks for a fortnight in advance of December 1, on which date the taxes actually become due."

The *Daily Standard* of December 8, 1885, has a long article commending and detailing Collector Tanner's improved methods. It is too long to quote entire, but a few excerpts will show its gist:

"The success of the plan originated by Tax Collector Tanner in accommodating the public in the matter of paying their yearly taxes has been more marked this year than ever before. The amount of taxes paid the first day, when Corporal Tanner went in office, was $400,000. This was doubled the next year, and has gone on increasing until this year, when it is more than half a million in excess of last year."

The *Daily Times* of December 26, 1885, said:

"It is generally admitted that the city never had a better tax collector than James Tanner. The reforms he has introduced in the workings of the office have been widely appreciated, and the public, without distinction of party, have given repeated and tangible proofs of their satisfaction. If he must now give place to a Democrat, it may at least be hoped that his successor will be one who can be trusted to continue the administration of the office in the same line of business principles."

Upon the incoming of a Democratic city government in 1886 a strong effort was made to have Mr. Tanner retained in the office. General Isaac S. Catlin, who had been the unsuccessful candidate for the mayoralty against the Democratic nominee, said to a representative of the *Standard:*

"There are in Brooklyn from five to seven thousand veterans in the Posts of the Grand Army of the Republic, and there is not a Post in the city that would not pass resolutions warmly thanking Mr. Hardenburgh (the newly-appointed collector) in getting out in favor of a badly-maimed soldier if Mr. Tanner should be re-appointed to his present position. By common consent Tanner has made the best collector of taxes that any city in the United States ever had. Fifty-five millions of dollars have passed through his hands, and not one cent of this stupendous sum remains unaccounted for. Every Brooklyn taxpayer knows that he has vastly improved the system of collection."

But the exigencies of the political situation prevented the accomplishment of the popular wish to have him retained.

After his retirement from the collector's office Mr. Tanner was in constant demand on the lecture platform, his reputation as a public speaker, eloquent, logical and witty, having been firmly established, and the announcement of an address by "Corporal Tanner" was found to be about the best drawing card lyceum managers and Grand Army posts throughout the country could offer.

He was especially happy in his remarks and thoroughly in his element at the reunions of veteran soldiers, and there is no one that the "boys" would rather listen to.

At a meeting of New Hampshire veterans, held in August, 1885, he was present, and, of course, was called on "to speak a piece." His address was thus reported by the *Boston Globe:*

"Corporal Tanner began by referring to camp-fires and the soldier's life generally, and to the time 'When Johnny came marching home.' He then described in a facetious way soldiers' fare, the troubles they used to have in baking 'hoe cakes,' which were so often allowed to burn up before the fire, through the knavery of some envious outsider who would manage to distract the attention of the cook at the critical moment, and so ruin what he could not share in. He then made passing allusions to certain raids on hen-roosts, of which he had heard, but requested his hearers not to judge the boys too harshly for little failings of this kind. They simply wished in a quiet way to keep down the enormous expenses of the Commissary Department. 'After a liberal dispensation of salt pork and hard tack,' he said, 'for an indefinite length of time, it is not to be supposed that a hungry soldier wants to have any conscientious scruples as to the remarkable longevity attained by a well-fattened chicken. Yes, we all own up after a while. Some would rather go into a fight than eat. I would rather eat.'

"The speaker then went on to relate the story of Malvern Hill, giving a description of the field, paying just tribute to the valor of the 'Johnny Rebs,' as they charged up again and again to the very mouths of the guns. He also related the anecdote of the rabbit which, affrighted by the uproar all around it, fled at the top of its speed across the front to the security of a distant woods, and as it was disappearing over the brow of a hill a gallant young officer, who was gazing after it with longing eyes, burst out: 'Go it, old cotton-tail! If it was n't for the looks of the thing I'd be with you!'

"It may be that some people think and say that this soldier business is played out. This, no well-informed person will acknowledge, for the spirit that actuates the boys now is the same that inspired them to march, to suffer, to fight, when their valor was all that stood between their country and ruin."

He was no less a favorite on the stump, and his ability as an orator, his intense, infectious earnestness and loyalty to the principles of the Republican party, made his services eagerly sought for in every political campaign during that stirring period. In 1886 he stumped the State of California for Mr. Swift, candidate for Governor. In 1887 he went through Oregon like a cyclone, and the Republican victory there was largely owing to his labors.

During the Presidential campaign of that year his eloquent voice was heard through the length and breadth of Indiana in impassioned appeals to the soldiers to rally to the support of General Harrison and the Republican candidate for Governor, Alvin P. Hovey, and he contributed in no small measure to their successful canvass.

Upon the inauguration of President Harrison there seemed to be a general consensus of opinion, especially among the soldiers, as to the proper person to take the responsible office of Commissioner of Pensions under the new administration. It seemed to belong to this maimed defender of his country, whose long service on the National Pension Committee of the Grand Army of the Republic, added to his legal knowledge and admitted ability, rendered him, in popular estimation, peculiarly fitted for its important duties.

He was appointed Commissioner of Pensions by President Harrison, March 23, 1889, and here he found a new and acceptable field for the exercise of his energy, enthusiasm and talents. Thoroughly sympathizing with the disabled victims of the War for the Union, he yet determined to construe the pension laws with strict and even-handed justice. What his personal feelings were may be gathered from a rather celebrated address he made at Columbia, Tenn., soon after his appointment. Speaking of the policy to be pursued he said:

"For long years I have had one conscientious conviction in my heart, which has grown with the years, and which is stronger to-day than ever before, namely, that it is the bounden duty of this great Republic of ours to see to it that no man who wore the blue and laid it off in honor shall ever be permitted to crawl under the roof of an alms-house for shelter."

And again :

"Within the limitations of the law, with due regard to my official oath, I here broadly assert that everything I can do to assist the needy and suffering veterans shall be done."

The popular approval of Mr. Tanner's selection as Commissioner of Pensions was universal and widespread. A few extracts from that "pulse of the people," the Press, will show this.

The Chicago *Inter-Ocean* said :

"The Commissioner of Pensions is a man who has made the pension system the study of the best years of his life, and who is supremely desirous to apply it to the benefit of those for whose aid it was devised. It is much to have a Department administered by a chief who is desirous that the object for which it was established shall be accomplished by it."

The San Francisco *Chronicle:*

"The new Commissioner seems to be taking hold of his work understandingly, and will make an efficient and valuable officer."

The Milwaukee *Sentinel:*

"The new Commissioner of Pensions is thoroughly in sympathy with the veterans. He has shown himself in every act he has performed a sincere friend of the soldiers."

The New York *Tribune:*

"Corporal Tanner, the new Commissioner of Pensions, has already instituted several salutary reforms."

The Troy *Times:*

"The way in which Commissioner Tanner dispatches the business of the Pension Department is commended on all sides, particularly among the Grand Army veterans."

The *Grand Army Gazette:*

"The *Grand Army Gazette* receives with pleasure the announcement of the appointment of Comrade James Tanner to the highly honorable position of Commissioner of Pensions, and begs to tender to him its very hearty congratulations," etc.

The National Tribune addressed him an open letter of congratulation, from which this sentence is quoted :

" Your appointment was a recognition of the widespread esteem of your comradeship and of the unmistakable desire of the veterans all over the country that you be put in charge of the administration of the Nation's justice to her soldiers."

And so it went all over the country. Mr. Tanner "buckled down" to the great work before him with that tremendous, cheerful energy that always characterized him. In the first six weeks of his administration nearly 20,000 pension certificates were issued, a gain of over 4,000 above the corresponding period of the previous year.

And just here comes in a little "bit" of Mr. Tanner's home life that is delightful and thoroughly characteristic. After a couple of months' siege of hotel life and "the incessant appearance of the bell boys with visitors' cards" when he was expecting a little relief from the cares of the day, he broke out gleefully as a school boy to a correspondent of one of the Brooklyn papers :

" My wife has at last decided to take the old Weaver mansion on Georgetown Heights, and I am more relieved than I can tell you. The place has some great advantages. There are three acres of ground and I can keep a lot of dogs. This will render it rather difficult of access to the average office-seeker. Since I have been at the head of the Pension Bureau I have had scarcely any time to myself, and I really could not stand the constant strain. The Weaver place is most delightfully situated; the air is cool, pleasant and healthy, and we shall move in as soon as some repairs are concluded, and the sooner we get there the better satisfied both Mrs. Tanner and myself will be."

It is doubtful, however, whether the change gave him much relief, for as one of his friends said: "They left the latch-string hanging out, and it would n't be Jim Tanner's house if they did n't."

One affecting incident that occurred early in Mr. Tanner's administration was connected with the troubles of the New York City Agency for paying pensions, in charge of Gen. Franz Sigel. The circumstances are familiar enough to newspaper readers and it is not necessary to detail them. General Sigel, himself the soul of honor, was technically responsible for the misdeeds of a subordinate, and tendered his resignation to Commissioner Tanner, who assured him that the matter in question did not reflect upon his honesty.

"I tell you," said the Commissioner, relating the occurrence, "it was pathetic. I could remember how General Sigel's horse had splashed mud over me as I stood in the ranks and he galloped along the line with his splendid staff in the old heroic days, and now here he was, a broken old man, offering me his resignation of an honorable and lucrative office. But I want the people to understand that General Sigel's personal record in the Pension Office is clean."

As the summer wore on the attacks of the opponents of Commissioner Tanner grew in violence. His resolve to cut red tape in the adjudication of meritorious claims; his indignant denunciation of the paltry stipends of one, two and three dollars per month doled out to disabled veterans, and his avowed determination to reissue the certificates of those unfortunates upon a more liberal basis, as was within his legal discretion, aroused a host of powerful enemies, not confined, it may be suggested, to one political party. As it was a pretty dull season anyhow, barren of any exciting subject for treatment, the newspapers entered into the discussion of his methods and plans with ardor (too often assumed). He was specially accused of having nefarious designs, for the benefit of the ex-soldiers, upon the mysterious "surplus" in the Treasury, that was a cause of much worriment to many editors and politicians who had none of their own. Then his noted Columbia, Tenn., speech, delivered May, 1889, added to the excitement in various quarters, and was made the subject of comment, friendly or otherwise, by almost every newspaper in the country. As this was probably the most important address Mr. Tanner made, at least during his incumbency of a Federal office, extracts sufficient to show its general spirit and tenor are appended.

Delivered before a distinctively Southern audience, its beauty of diction and sentiment, the fervid eloquence of its delivery, and the manly sympathy of the orator with the "maimed victims of the Lost Cause, sitting in the solitude of their wrecked and ruined homes," created a profound sensation through the entire country, and its echoes may be yet heard among the dwellers in the deep forests, by the lonely lagoons and on the broad plantations of the far South, who had borne arms for the Confederacy.

"Friends and countrymen," he commenced, "we thank God and congratulate ourselves, as we assemble here to-day, that there is so much in our possession and so much in prospect for us in common as citizens of this great Republic. And without regard to the boundaries of any particular State which we designate as our own, we look back over a hundred years that are passed and gone, and we see much of struggle, much of creation, much of bitter sectionalism, and all too much, we will all agree, in the last quarter-century, of bloody strife. Thank God, we can contemplate it as of the past, and, we firmly believe, the forever past. Standing to-day upon the shining uplands of prosperity and peace, we sweep the world with our gaze, and contemplate with pride the fact that the American nation stands secure, its position unchallenged in the face of the civilized world, the glory of its citizenship respected and honored in the four quarters of the earth. But a peculiar combination of circumstances encompass, while they do not embarrass, me to-day, and seem to indicate that there are some lines of thought and speech to which my mind should fitly turn.

"Within the time of those of us who are now of middle or elder age, this country has been shaken from center to circumference by the

RUDE SHOCK OF BLOODY WAR;

of war in its most horrible form; a death struggle between brethren of the same household. Here to-day are assembled many men who in the memorable struggle of 1861 to 1865, contested on the one side for the disruption, and on the other for the preservation of the Union.

"If there be any fitness in my appearance on this platform to-day it arises from the fact that in the days of that struggle I stood in the ranks of that mighty column of blue. If there are any words to which my tongue can most appropriately turn to give utterance to-day, they should formulate themselves into a message which I feel I can honestly, conscientiously and consistently bring from my comrades of the North, who in the years of our strife, in answer to the defiance of the old time and never-to-be-forgotten 'rebel yell,' sent ringing back to the extent of our lung power the Yankee hurrah. If there be any class of citizens over this whole country with whose sentiments I am familiar above that of any other class, it is

THE VETERANS

of the Union Armies who, from 1861 to 1865, when health was in their faces and vigor in their steps, belted the country across with a line of blue and beat back the mighty hosts of the South; and I am proud of the fact that I can bring from my comrades of the North-land a sentiment in perfect harmony with the peace and pleasantry and good feeling which is such an adjunct on this occasion to-day. If I may be pardoned a personal reference, then permit me to say that I am also proud of the fact the sentiments of my heart are, and for long, long years have been, utterly in accord with the unification and homogenity of the exercises of this hour.

"Very many years ago I stated, have repeated it many times since then, meant it every time I repeated it, and mean it to-day no less than ever, that if there should walk into my office the 'Johnnie' who pulled the lanyard of the gun which sent the shell that crippled me for life, and I was satisfied that he stood with me to-day for the honor of our common institutions and the glory of our common flag, this right hand would reach way out across the so-called bloody chasm, and I would say: 'Put it there, Johnnie; you and I will go out and take dinner together and talk over old times.'

"The fact of the business is that when Lee surrendered to Grant at Appomattox no two classes of men were more nearly together, not only physically, but mentally, than the two lines of men who stood there, one dressed in gray and one in blue. All true men know this, that no matter how earnestly you may fight a man, no matter how utterly you may condemn the principles for which he contends, when you find that man so terribly in earnest that he offers his life in behalf of the principles for which he combats, a respect grows up for that mighty earnestness in spite of our utmost antagonism to the principles he contends for.

"You will bear in mind that I am speaking of the men who fought, not of those who never fronted the shock of war, and did not get mad until all opportunity to do battle had passed away. They are the fellows who yelled themselves into an advanced stage of bronchitis asking 'Why don't the army move?' and who no sooner heard the call for three hundred thousand more than they at once came to a position of "rest," with a draft list in one hand and a time-table of the nearest route to Canada in the other, ready to skip across the border if their names appeared among those who were drawn for service."

Speaking of his duties as Commissioner of Pensions, Mr. Tanner said:

"For long years I have had one conscientious conviction in my heart which has grown with the years and is stronger to-day than ever before, namely, that it is the bounden duty of this great Republic of ours to see to it that no man who wore the blue and laid it off in honor, shall ever feel the necessity of, or be permitted, to crawl under the roof of an almshouse for shelter."

He added:

"Let me put the question to them, and I will go under bond that the men who aided in the defense of the Confederacy will give a unanimous vote in the affirmative to the proposition that, not only in common decency and the natural promptings of the human heart, but the best and highest exposition of wise political economy demands that the boys who are growing up to-day must not see the defenders of the Union, who in the past held life so cheap and their country so dear that they freely flung life as a willing offering in its defense, permitted to go hungry or in rags."

Speaking of the 33,000 pensioners drawing less than one dollar a week, he remarked: " I mean to put these up to four dollars a month, though I may wring from the hearts of some the prayer, 'God help the surplus.'"

After referring to the order he issued on Memorial Day, when he was Department Commander of New York State, in which he expressed the hope that the Comrades would drop a wreath on the graves of such of the boys of the South as had found a sepulchre among us, he continued:

" Later on there came to us the cry of the stricken and the maimed, and it was my high privilege, and my halting footsteps made speed to obey the willing dictates of my heart, as we called together the citizens of that great City of Churches, for a score of years my home, and it was my privilege to present a plea for the veterans of the South. We of the North had the coffers of the Treasury to draw upon for our pensions; we had honor among the nations of the earth, but I stated that the man who followed the fortunes of the Confederacy and who had also been maimed, sat in the solitude of his wrecked and ruined home and contemplated, possibly, loss of limb, and saw his wife in rags and his child in hunger, and that as we were human and bowed before a common God, it remained for us to see that in all the desolation and want and misery that came to his hearthstone, there should not also come loss of faith in humanity."

Speaking again of his official duties as he saw them, he said:

"I am clearly of the opinion that I voice the dominant sentiment of this country when I unhesitatingly declare that a wise policy demands that in treating with those who have just claims before this country I should cease to hunt for merely technical reasons with which to defeat them, and devote a little time, at least, to helping those claimants who in the past did not hesitate to help the country in its hour of dire peril. Within the limitations of the law, with due regard to my official oath, I here broadly assert that everything that I can do to assist the needy and suffering veterans shall be done."

After declaring that it was the solemn duty of the Southern States to enact such laws as would provide for the maimed and disabled ex-Confederates, he closed with an eloquent and touching peroration, trusting that, when the call shall be sounded for the last assembly, on the farther shore, the Blue and the Gray would be found together in the ranks commanded by the Prince of Peace.

On the 12th of September, 1889, Mr. Tanner forwarded his resignation to the President in a manly, straight-forward letter, which needs no explanation. It was as follows:

"DEPARTMENT OF THE INTERIOR,
"BUREAU OF PENSIONS,
"WASHINGTON, D. C., *September 12, 1889.*

"*To the President:*

"The difference which exists between the Secretary of the Interior and myself as to policy to be pursued in the administration of the Pension Bureau has reached a stage which threatens to embarrass you to an extent which I feel I should not call upon you to suffer, and as the investigation into the affairs of the Bureau has been completed and, I am assured by yourself and the Secretary of the Interior, it contains no reflection on myself whether as an individual or an officer, I hereby place my resignation in your hands, to take effect at your pleasure, to the end that you may be relieved of any further embarrassment in the matter.

"Very respectfully yours,
"JAMES TANNER,
"*Commissioner.*"

The President replied as follows:

"EXECUTIVE MANSION,
"WASHINGTON, *September 13, 1889.*
"*To the Honorable James Tanner,
Commissioner of Pensions:*

"*Dear Sir:* Your letter tendering the offer of your resignation of the office of Commissioner of Pensions has been received, and your resignation is accepted to take effect on the appointment and qualification of your successor.

"I do not think it necessary in this correspondence to discuss the causes which have led to the present attitude of affairs in the Pension Office. You have been kindly and fully advised of my views upon most of these matters.

"It gives me pleasure to add that, so far as I am advised, your honesty has not at any time been called in question, and I beg to renew the expression of my personal good will.

"Very truly yours,
"BENJAMIN HARRISON."

Mr. Tanner's resignation, and the causes leading to it, caused wide-spread comment. The papers from Maine to California were full of it, and naturally, the views expressed varied greatly, according to the sentiments, feelings and prejudices of the writers.

Among the prominent men interviewed upon the subject was General B. F. Butler, who, not to be misunderstood, wrote out in his own incisive style, his opinion on the merits of the case as follows:

* * * "The Commissioners, as a rule, have looked upon a pension as something in the nature of a bounty, which was to be given to the soldier as a gratuity; that it was a charge on the Government, and that, like every other charge against the Government, a man, to get it, must do everything he is called upon to do, to prove every fact that he is called upon to prove beyond doubt, and make such proof of the case as would be a necessity in a court of justice. It was, therefore, the rule that he must take two comrades to swear to his original disability, or one commissioned officer to certify to this disability. Why that rule? There is nothing in the law about it, but it has been the rule of the Office.

"Everything else in the world, except how a soldier became injured, could be proved by the oath of one good man, the crime of perjury could be established by the oath of one good man, but the rule of the Pension Office was that it must take the oath of *two* of his comrades, and the effect was, if a man could not find two of his comrades, or one commissioned officer, to prove how he got hurt and where, and whether he was in line of duty, he was deprived of his pension. The distinction between officers and men in regard to truth telling I do not believe ought to exist. Again, the feeling has been created that everything that was gotten out of the Treasury was so much taken from the people of the United States, and that everything should be done to prevent its being gotten out. Every doubt was against the pension, never the benefit of a doubt given the soldier. The Pension Office was administered according to a rule of Hoyle—'When in doubt, take the trick.'

"One of the *most benificent* as well as the most just

acts of Commissioner Tanner is that he has abolished that rule that it takes two volunteers to prove a comrade's disability and only one commissioned officer. [It was so regarded by just men all over the United States, and cases which, for lack of that second comrade's testimony, when it was impossible to get it, but which contained the affidavit of one good and true man, cases which had lain from fifteen to twenty years in the archives of the Pension Office, and the applicant suffering through the years for the necessities of life, were taken out of their dusty receptacles and acted upon, some completed, others were being pushed to that end. Two weeks after Mr. Tanner's retirement from office the order was revoked and all those cases ordered back to their long resting place.—J. E. S.] His critics say he has no discrimination. Well, he had discrimination enough to know that his own certificate to a comrade's wounds ought to weigh as much as that of anyone else, yet by that rule he would have to get somebody else, also, to certify, to give a pension to a man he saw shot down by his side. He did not mean to serve under any such disability as that, and I am sure every right-feeling man will say amen.

"Again he believes that in a case proven beyond a reasonable doubt, the pension should be granted. To illustrate what I mean—the rules of the Office on the subject of marriage, when I had to do with them, were against the law, and different from every State in the Union. By the decision of the Supreme Court, the fact that a man and woman live together in a form of marriage and are so known and reputed, is a proof that they are man and wife, unless something is shown to the contrary. All States have a law that in case of a divorce either to be obtained or to be resisted, cohabitation as man and wife is sufficient evidence of marriage. But the rule of the Pension Office has been that a soldier's widow must produce the certificate of some one who married them, or produce the record of her marriage and the evidence of her identity with the person who was married, or a witness who was present at the marriage—no matter how long she may have lived with her husband or how many children she may have borne him, who have grown up to be held in honor as sons of veterans—before she can get a pension, in case her husband dies, and her husband's certificate to the fact of their marriage, or his will in favor of his wife were not evidence in the Pension Office. Thousands and thousands of soldiers' widows have been denied a pension on these technical rules, that are not in use or required in any court of justice on a trial of marriage.

"For what reason? Why, that there are bad women who pretend to be married when they are not. Would *I* pay such women pensions if they were *not* married? No, not if I knew it, not if it were so shown to me. But I would act in regard to them under the pension laws as everybody acts under every other law, and if I made a mistake, I should rather it be in favor of the woman. If she has taken care of, and rendered comfortable, the soldier in his sickness and old age, and tended his grave, I should not be so very much troubled as to whether there was a ceremony prior to that or not, if she acted as his wife. Oh, but I would deplete the Treasury, would I? Well, I would not have any trouble on that account, I would a great deal rather deplete the Treasury that way, than by putting it into Englishmen's pockets by a free-trade tariff. To get the surplus out of the Treasury, we are buying up bonds and making a little profit out of the speculation, so as to get the money into circulation, and to keep it from being locked up in the Treasury. Is there any better way on earth to distribute the money gotten out of the Treasury, than to give it to poor pensioners, who pay it out at once to 'the butcher, the baker and candlestick maker,' and everybody else, before it gets into a bank, or into an accumulation of money?

"Whereas, when they buy bonds it goes directly into

the hands of the capitalist, and enables him to foster great trusts, which make provisions dearer, and puts a tax upon the necessities of life. No such thing happens when the money is paid the pensioner.

"Mr. Tanner has not gone so far as I would have gone in his place, is all I can say. The only difference, otherwise, between us would have been, that I, being an old politician and used to being vilified, and being reasonably strong in body, with my legs to walk upon, would not have been rendered a little peevish by my pain, and should have heard all my opponents had to say, without caring a copper, and without reply. The soldier, wounded and suffering, stung to death by the spiders and gnats and mosquitoes of the Press, did reply, and that is brought up against him. They say it was not in good taste. I never heard he did not fight in good taste when he shot the enemies of his country. It is nothing to me, whether his rifle was clean or dirty in the Rebellion, and it is just as little to me now, when he shoots at the enemies of his country in peace, whether his words are exactly as rhetorical as they would have been had he in 1861 gone to college instead of to battle. I think he made the better Commissioner that he went to battle instead of to college.

"Well, of what do they accuse him? Does anybody say he has given the money of the Government to anybody who was not a soldier in the War of the Rebellion? Why, it is said he has given pensions to soldiers who had not an honorable discharge. But that was not his ruling; *that* was the ruling of the Assistant Secretary of the Interior, and I am quite sure he is not right. The country promised everybody a pension who went to the war, was injured and had an honorable discharge. If he deserted, and so did not get an honorable discharge, the penalty by law for that was death, if the Government chose to enforce it. But you will search in vain for loss of pension on that account. But what the Assistant Secretary of the Interior decided regarding this is of very little account so far as Mr. Tanner is concerned. He only followed the decision of his superior.

* * * "To the honor of the Confederates be it spoken that no complaint of Mr. Tanner's course comes up from the South. There may be now and then some Yankee who has wandered down there, and got some newspaper to say something about it, but from the Confederate soldier nothing is said. In the political organizations of the South—Southern men—nothing is said. It is only the worst enemies that the country had in its struggles for its life—the Copperheads of the North—that are against the Grand Army, and against Corporal Tanner.

'The mower mows on, though the adder may writhe
And the copperhead curl round the blade of the scythe.'

"About re-rating, those cases re-rated by Corporal Tanner. A law was passed that they should be re-rated, not long before the late Commissioner Black went out of office. That law was executed by him faithfully, fully, and generously, and I never heard of any body that complained about the manner in which it was executed. And it will turn out, I have no doubt, that after the law was passed, in the latter part of General Black's administration, he re-rated and raised more pensions, and raised them higher than Corporal Tanner has done. At any rate, let any commission of investigation take that into account.

"Does anybody complain that Mr. Tanner has done anything more than his duty, done it diligently, has been restless in the good work? He ought indeed to be commended for doing justice *according to the laws that Congress has passed* to his poor, bleeding, dying comrades. Let any *soldier* cast the first stone and then a mugwump may follow with a bad egg."

Among the numerous public expressions of sympathy tendered to Mr. Tanner on this occasion probably none affected him more than the resolution unanimously adopted by the Genesee Methodist Conference Veteran

Association at Lockport, N. Y. This Association is composed of ministers who saw active service at the front during the war, and the resolution, adopted without a dissenting voice was as follows:

"*Resolved*, That we have heard with sincere regret of the resignation as Commissioner of Pensions of Corporal James Tanner, forced from him by the influence of politicians, and that we deprecate the subordination of the pension department to political wirepullers so that it can not be administered by a man who, like Corporal Tanner, has the true interests of the soldiers at heart; and we call upon the President of the United States to place the granting of pensions in the hands of those who will administer it in the interests of those who fought, bled and suffered for their country, and to bestow upon Corporal Tanner recognition as befits the man who, in every position, has shown himself the true friend of the soldier."

After his retirement from the Pension Bureau, Mr. Tanner entered upon the practice of his profession in Washington and has built up an excellent business.

He still resides in picturesque old Georgetown, and has a most delightful home, presided over by his accomplished wife, a lady thoroughly fitted to be his helper and inspiration, and brightened by two charming young daughters, and a pair of sturdy sons.

Corporal Tanner is in the prime of his manhood, vigorous, alert and ambitious, and it needs no prophet to predict that he will yet be prominent in the councils of the Nation. He is a man with a future as well as a glorious past, and his career, here imperfectly sketched, is not closed. "All things come to him who waits," and when the opportunity arrives the man will be found ready.
JAMES E. SMITH.

EARLY DAYS IN THE BLACK HILLS

The explorations of Professor Jenny and General Custer during the years 1874 and 1875 in that wild upheaval of the earth's surface known as the Black Hills of Dakota, resulted in their purchase by the Government. Long before the completion of the treaty, however, by which this tract was acquired from its aboriginal inhabitants, organized bands of "prospectors" were on hand, hovering along the borderland, much as in later years attended the opening up of Oklahoma. But the Black Hills had been for ages the hunting ground of numerous bands of restless, untamable savages, who recognized no right in the Sioux chiefs to transfer these lands, and they openly declared that they would lift the scalp of every white man they caught in their domain.

This was not a pleasant outlook for the gold-hunters, but, while mostly unskilled in Indian warfare, they were as a rule bold, reckless men, not unused to taking desperate chances, so when the military let down the bars a great horde rushed in, the most of whom succeeded in reaching Custer City. This was a post established by General Custer, and consisted of log barracks and, some distance down the valley of French Creek, a stockade erected by Professor Jenny. The first comers put up tents and rough log shanties, and so the infant city was started. The roving Indians promptly opened hostilities by blockading the only two roads leading into the Hills from the south, one through the Red Cañon, the other by way of Buffalo Gap. Red Cañon became a veritable valley of death. Train after train was captured, the freighters slaughtered and their goods carried away or burned. As the young city and the adjacent mining camps depended on these trains for supplies, the situation was rapidly becoming desperate. Outside, grim death awaited all stragglers, while in the city the prospect of starvation was disagreeably imminent.

We had the usual supply of alleged desperadoes with us in that trying time—"Red-handed Mike" and "Arapahoe Joe" and numerous others with blood-curdling nick-names, who adorned the saloons, and with huge revolvers strapped to their hips, made the air blue with details of the sanguinary deeds they had done and could do, but not one of them volunteered to go out on the trail or venture their worthless carcasses beyond the danger line for the protection of the trains. In this desperate strait a meeting was called in Custer to consider what was best to do. Among those present was a quiet, unassuming young man who had seen service in the Civil War, and enjoyed the unique distinction, in that part of the country, of having never tasted liquor

J. W. CRAWFORD

in his life, nor gambled, nor was he given to profane relations of his own wonderful exploits; yet he was pretty well known as a man of iron nerve, sound judgment, and a courage that no danger could appall. About the only concession he made to the established customs of the plains was in allowing his abundant brown hair to float down his shoulders in silky waves, and in wearing a great, wide-brimmed, felt hat. His handsome features and soft blue eyes, with a dreamy cast of countenance, rendered him a remarkable man in any gathering. His gentle, courteous manners, however, were never misunderstood by the desperate characters so plentiful on the border. They treated him with the respect that his record warranted. This was Capt. Jack Crawford, who later on commanded Crook's scouts.

With rather unexpected good judgment the meeting decided to appeal to Captain Jack, whose headquarters were then in Custer City, to take charge of the situation, with full powers. He accepted the responsibility, and an immediate change for the better became apparent. He and his band of trained scouts soon taught the fierce Arabs of the plains to keep out of their reach, and so vigilantly did they guard the trails that an unwonted sense of security pervaded the city and surrounding camps. The trains came through with reasonable regularity, and provisions became plentiful. Rifles and revolvers were no longer considered necessary bed-fellows, and I can recall with what a comfortable feeling of security I would lie down in my bunk at night when I knew that Jack and his faithful troop were out on the road between us and the savages.

But this peaceful state of affairs did n't last a great

while. General Crook's column came along and absorbed Captain Crawford and his gallant scouts. With their disappearance on that long campaign our troubles recommenced.

Our wily foes resumed their bloody work, and just beyond Custer City there seemed to be an invisible dead line — whoever crossed it never returned. His bones alone were afterwards found on the arid desert.

The passage of the Red Cañon again became so fraught with peril that few were bold enough to attempt it. I recall the horror that thrilled us when we heard of the massacre of the Metz party of seven determined men who had made the venture. Not one lived to get through.

There was an irregular line of stages running between Cheyenne and the Hills. That is a coach, so called, would make the passage when it was considered safe to do so. After Captain Jack's departure the stages ceased their trips until one night a bold driver known as "Stuttering Brown" determined to try and get through. He carried no passengers. He had not gone many miles before he was attacked by the watchful savages, and lashing his animals to the top of their speed he kept up a running fight until, becoming desperately wounded, he mounted one of the mules, cut him loose from the stage and so escaped into Fort Laramie, where he died.

On the road which enters the Hills through Buffalo Gap matters were equally as bad. Incoming trains were corralled and attacked, the animals stampeded and supplies destroyed. The few that did reach us left many of their companions on the plains. Certain death awaited those who ventured beyond the foot-hills. A number of so-called "scouts" were engaged to replace Captain Crawford's band, but their services were of slight account.

A few incidents will serve to show the perilous character of the surroundings of the mining towns in the Hills. One Sunday early in June, 1876, a Rev. Dr. Smith preached a sermon to an attentive crowd on the only street in Deadwood. After concluding his discourse he started on foot and alone for Crook City, eight miles east, where he had promised to hold services. It was, of course, a rash undertaking, but he was a resolute, fearless man, and could not be persuaded to wait until a party would go over. He was killed and scalped within two miles of the spot where he had delivered his last sermon. When the news reached Deadwood a force was organized to go out and bring in his body, which they did, but at the cost of three more lives before sunset. The bodies were all brought in and buried in a newly-opened cemetery, since made famous by Capt. Jack Crawford in a poem dedicated to "Wild Bill."

One of the brave dead was Charley Holland, who had come out in our train. He was an Odd Fellow, and about seventy brothers of the Order, including this writer, were gathered together and followed his remains to their last resting place across the creek of Deadwood. Under the shadow of a tall cypress we laid him away, while Judge Kuykendall, of Cheyenne, read the burial service of the I. O. O. F.

While this ceremony was going on, a second party was performing the last sad rites for another of the victims, Ike Brown, who, although a professional gambler, had many manly qualities and an unflinching courage that extorted universal admiration. He died, at the least, in a good cause.

Meanwhile things were rapidly going from bad to worse, and finally the miners of Deadwood and vicinity took the bull by the horns as it were, and offered a reward of $300 for every Indian head brought in. The first (and the only one, I believe) that was presented created the wildest excitement in the camp. Business was suspended, the head elevated on a pole and carried up and down the gulch, followed by a frantic crowd, yelling like lunatics.

The man who had brought in the cause of all this commotion was the hero of the hour; nothing was too good for him. He owned the town. But he bore his blushing honors meekly, and modestly declined to talk much of his daring achievement.

The next morning, however, produced a startling change in the situation, at least for one man, in the shape of another "Richmond" in quest of a head that had been separated from the body of an Indian killed by him the day before while he was in pursuit of a small band that had stolen some horses from him. He did not stop until he had recovered his animals some distance below Crook City. When he returned to his "good Indian" he found the head missing. The wrath of the rancher may be imagined. He swore a mighty oath to slay the man who had played him such a scurvy trick. He soon got on his trail and tracked him to Deadwood. The meeting between them was sharp and decisive, and ended in the hero of the celebration of the day before biting the dust. Nothing was ever done to the ranchman, for the Deadwood of that period, rough as it was, had no use for a thief.

Early in June, I decided to leave Deadwood for civilization. On arriving at Custer City I had to wait several days until a train was made up for the trip to Cheyenne, as the chances of one man, or even two or three, reaching it were of the slimmest kind. A party of twenty-one men and ten wagons finally got ready, elected a Captain, one Glynn, to whom was delegated absolute authority over the outfit, and, by a majority vote, the route through Red Cañon was selected.

About this time, as we afterwards learned, the deserters from the Red Cloud and Spotted Tail Agencies were moving north to join Sitting Bull. Their trail crossed ours between the mouth of Red Cañon and "Down Indian" Creek.

The first station after leaving the Red Cañon is "Cheyenne River Ranch," and from there it is thirty-three miles to "Down Indian" Creek, the next station where wood and water was to be had. This is called "the long drive."

On this part of the route we found abundant evidence that a large force of braves had very recently passed to the north. We saw numerous ponies and troops of forlorn looking dogs straggling along, evidently in the wake of the advancing column. Our party captured a number of the ponies, that were secured by the men without going too far away from the train, for Indian "signs" were becoming alarmingly thick. We proceeded cautiously until about noon when we were halted by a fusilade from the crest of a bluff, which concealed the enemy from our view. The train was corralled and preparations made for defence.

After standing around for about an hour and hearing

nothing further from the enemy, I became impatient and asked the Captain what he intended doing. "Oh, we must wait for developments," was his reply.

Now my knowledge of Indian fighting was very limited, but it seemed to me that if the savages were strong enough to attack us they would have done so before this, and I so stated to the Captain, adding that if he would give me ten men, half the force, I would deploy them as skirmishers and find out the exact situation of affairs. He flatly refused.

Meantime the firing from the bluff had re-commenced and stray bullets were dropping unpleasantly near, liable to do damage any minute, while twenty armed men were hugging the ground inside the corral.

I tried to convince the party of the danger of remaining inactive, thus giving the Indians time to collect a force large enough to overwhelm us, but all to no purpose.

Becoming thoroughly exasperated, I leaped on my horse and dashed straight for the bluffs, where I had just seen two heads cautiously raised to take observations. As I neared the hills I noticed a gap, caused by a dry creek or ravine, on the left, and making for it at a run, I flanked the bluff and was rewarded by seeing two braves in hasty retreat! This, of course, increased my courage, and dashing across the sandy bed of the creek I fired two or three shots in quick succession after the flying foe. Just then my horse stumbled and threw me over his head. I had a pretty hard fall, but recovered myself and started back, leading the horse. I expected that at least a few of my brave companions would have come to my assistance, but not one of them had moved from the safe covert of the corral. I was sore from the fall, and deeply chagrined by the womanish timidity of the men I was traveling with through this dangerous country, and when I got back to them I expressed my views of their conduct in no measured terms. They took the rating meekly enough, and the Captain, feeling that he was out of his element, resigned his charge. I was immediately elected to the vacancy, but promptly declined the honor. I curtly informed the gang that I had no doubt of my ability to reach Cheyenne, but doubted very much whether they would ever see it.

The next night we camped at Hat Creek, where we met a detachment of soldiers who had been sent out to help the ranchers, whose property had been destroyed by the Indians on their march to the Little Big Horn. A sutler, who was with the troops, had a generous supply of whiskey, and the members of our train clubbed together and purchased some twenty half-pint flasks, which were solemnly tendered to me as a peace-offering! I declined the testimonial, and as we reached Laramie soon after, I there left the outfit and rode into Cheyenne, ninety-three miles, alone.

Several days later, while seated in a barber's chair enjoying a civilized shave, I was treated to a thrilling tale of the wild adventures of a small party that had just come in from the Black Hills. The individual who was giving his experience of the desperate fight his train had had—how they were compelled to entrench on the prairie; how a mere handful of brave men had, after a long and bloody struggle, beat off a vastly superior body of Indians—was behind me and I could not see his face. When the barber had completed his job I turned to ask this gallant hero where he and his party had been rounded up, and was struck speechless at beholding one of our own party, a freighter named Harris, who had never showed his nose outside the corral while the *two* Indians remained on the bluffs.

When he saw me he collapsed at once, but recovering himself he declared to the crowd that I had saved the train by my personal prowess. I was pretty wrathy, and nipped the blood-curdling story in the bud by relating the actual facts of the case, which were tame enough. When I had got through the freighter had disappeared and I saw no more of him or his companions.

I may be pardoned for relating here a few little incidents connected with Captain Crawford.

When General Crook and his famished army reached Deadwood on their return, they had been subsisting on horse-flesh for many days prior to their arrival. Captain Jack had promised the correspondent of the New York *Herald* to deliver his dispatches at the nearest telegraph office in advance of his competitors, and so hurried on ahead of the army at his utmost speed. He came into Deadwood in advance of the column—to arrange for his eighty-mile ride to Custer and thence to Laramie. He was, needless to say, very hungry, and carried with him his share of the last army rations issued—a hind leg of a colt! Entering the "I. X. L." hotel he slapped his meat on the counter and requested the man in charge to have a steak cooked from that, quick.

Jack had just come off a long and fatiguing campaign, part of the time hunting Indians, and a considerable portion of it being hunted by them. He was weary and haggard, his hair unkempt and face covered with a beard an inch long, and although no man was better known in Deadwood and the mining camps around it, it was not strange that the barkeeper failed to recognize the pleasant-mannered pioneer scout of the Black Hills in the wild looking individual who wanted a steak prepared from the leg of a colt.

Keeping an eye on his suspicious customer, he backed off towards the kitchen, separated from the bar and dining room by a screen door. Through this he plunged rather precipitately, almost upsetting the proprietor, Jimmy Van Danniker, who was coming in from the kitchen.

"What the devil ails you?" he shouted.

"There's a wild man at the counter who wants a horse cooked!" gasped the barkeeper.

Van Danniker cautiously reconnoitered the situation, and, slipping behind the bar, secured his revolver and then sternly demanded of the uncouth object before him an explanation. Jack, who had laid his weary head on his folded arms was half asleep, but at the summons raised up and looked his old friend full in the face, but could discern no answering glance of recognition in the angry eyes that glared threateningly at him. Van was known to be, in the Hills vernacular, "a bad man with a gun," and unpleasantly quick sometimes to resent any "fooling," to use another expressive term, so Crawford just quietly said, "Jim, don't you know me?"

The musical voice was about all that was left of Jack, seemingly, but it was enough. Down went the revolver, out of the front door the leg of the colt, and Captain Jack soon sat down to a repast that included the best of everything in the Deadwood market.

After filling up to the limit, and a short rest, he pulled out for Custer City, urging his wiry little broncho to its utmost speed. Upon his arrival, just before dark, the horse was so utterly worn out that he found himself compelled to lay over and give it a chance to recuperate. He placed him in a stall next to one occupied by a famous race horse owned by a well-known sporting man from Denver, named Davis, who happened to be in Custer City, and knowing Jack intimately, had offered him the use of his stable.

Returning to the cabin dignified by the name of hotel, he rolled himself in his blanket on the floor of an empty room and would have been instantly asleep had he not overheard a few words of conversation, from a party in the adjoining room, in which his own name occurred. Listening with the trained intensity of a frontiersman, he discovered that a scheme had been formed by the other newspaper correspondents at Custer to get their dispatches in ahead of Jack. They had engaged a well-known mail-rider to carry their matter, with the understanding that if he succeeded in reaching a telegraph station in advance of Crawford his compensation would be something princely. After the business had been disposed of the party separated, the mail-rider stipulating that he should have a couple of hours' sleep before starting.

"Jack's broncho is used up, anyhow," he remarked. "I've looked him over, and he can't stir before morning, if then."

This was enough for Captain Jack, and waiting until he heard his rival snoring, he silently crept out, and going to the stable he felt around in the dark for his horse. To his intense dismay he found him lying in in the stall dead. This was a state of affairs he had not counted upon. Where to get another animal at that hour he did not know, and delay meant defeat, for the mail-rider was undoubtedly well equipped for his trip.

Jack had a well-written account of Crook's great campaign to its termination, but its special value depended upon his getting it telegraphed to the *Herald* ahead of the rival news-gatherers.

Just then the Davis mare neighed.

"Aha! said Jack softly, "that settles it." And in a few minutes he had her saddled and bridled, led out and mounted.

Walking her cautiously past the house, he suddenly found himself, in the dim light, looking into the muzzle of a Henry rifle protruding from an open window, with Davis' grim face behind it!

"Don't shoot, Davis!" he cried. "It's I—Jack Crawford. I'll take good care of the mare and bring her back to you, but I must have her to-night," and he was off on the trail like the wind. Davis did n't shoot, although that mare was the apple of his eye, for he knew that he could trust Jack.

That long, solitary, and dangerous ride through a desert, peopled only by roving bands of hostile savages; the arrival the next day at Laramie; the holding of the wires (after the despatches had been sent off), with a mass of personal adventures, against the delayed matter of the other correspondents until he felt assured (which turned out to be a fact) that the New York *Herald* had the exclusive details of the campaign a day in advance of any other paper in America, all this has been published heretofore and need not be repeated.

The *Herald* was so pleased with the exploit that its proprietor sent Jack a check high up in three figures, and his thanks besides.

Captain Crawford has collected and published his poems in an elegant volume, which has had a wide sale. With his permission one of them, a dialect poem, is here given. It is an excellent example of his versatility and of the sparkling wit that bubbles from his pen as naturally and refreshingly as the cool waters from some mountain spring. It originally appeared in the New York *Clipper*.

Santa Claus in the Mines.

It seemed so tarnal foolish like
    Fur men ter tackle children's play,
But w'en ol' Californy Mike
    Said: "Boys, to-morrow 's Christmas day;
Suppose we all hang up our socks
    An' see what Sandy Claws 'll bring?"
Us four, big, burly miner gawks
    Decided it war jest the thing.

So thar, beside our cabin fire,
    All glowin' with its ruddy coals,
We made a play, but I 'm a liar
    If every sock wan't full o' holes!
At this diskivery we all
    Roared out in laughin' shouts an' hoots,

Till Forty-niner Jim McCall
   Said: "Durn it, le 's hang up our boots."

The new suggestion seemed to strike
   The gang as bein' payin' ore,
So every boot went on a spike
   Drove jest outside the cabin door,
An' then fur two hull hours we set
   A talkin' Chris'mas talk, an' all
The boys a guessin' w'at they 'd get
   When Sandy made his flyin' call.

We talked of boyhood's happy times
   W'en Chris'mas cum, back in the States,
An' how we used ter save the dimes
   Ter buy our little sleds an' skates.
An' how the row of little socks
   'D hang above the fireplace light
An' all about our hopeful talks
   W'en in our trundle beds at night.

I 'll tell ye, pard, thar wa'nt no lack
   O' regular, outpourin' tears,
As recollection tuk us back
   Along the trail now dimmed with years.
An' every heart jest seemed to melt
   While talkin' of our kith and kin,
An' each ol' grizzled miner felt
   Jest like he war a boy agin.

Next mornin' jest as peep o' day
   Across the mountain 'gan ter drift,
As in our bunks we snoozin' lay,

One o' the boys yelled "Chris'mas Gift!"
Then up we sprung onto the floor,
　　A bilin' with ol' boyish fun,
An' made a rush out o' the door
　　Ter see w'at Sandy Claws had done.

*　　*　　*　　*　　*　　*

I 've heard o' men so cussed mean
　　They wa'nt fit ter live with hogs,
Nor wa'nt proper ter be seen
　　In company o' decent dogs.
But they war angels w'en compar'd
　　Unto that meanest o' galoots
Thet in the quiet night-time dar'd
　　Ter sneak along an' steal our boots!

A string o' tracks out through the snow,
　　Toward a distant minin' camp,
The thief's direction went to show,
　　An' indicated him a tramp.
But somehow in my mind it runs
　　'Twar Sandy Claws as tuk 'em in,
Ter punish us big sons of guns,
　　Fur tryin' ter be boys agin.

Capt. Crawford is of Scottish lineage, and doubtless some tinge of the Highland blood of his remote ancestry is responsible for his adventurous life. He enlisted early in the war in a company recruited about Minersville, Pa. His company was in the advance in the gigantic work of undermining the forts in front of Petersburg. He was twice wounded, once at Chancellorsville, and again at Spottsylvania, and a very slight limp in his gait serves as a reminder of his life at the front.

After the war he drifted to the West, and was one of the seven men who first penetrated the Black Hills, being chief of scouts for a party of rangers. He subsequently served with Custer, and then as chief of scouts for Gen. Crook. He afterwards took part in the campaign against the old Indian chief Victoria, following him to the Mexican line, where Victoria was killed.

Secretary Lincoln appointed him post trader at Fort Craig, New Mexico, after this campaign, and after that post was abandoned he was made custodian of the reservation.

He is now employed as a Special Agent of the Indian Bureau, looking up frauds against these wards of the Nation, and waging war against those selling them liquor.

His home is an ideal one for a borderman, being romantically situated on the banks of the Rio Grande, in the centre of his cattle range of forty-two miles square, where his herds of cattle and brood-mares roam at will in the wide river bottoms and through the grassy foothills. Here he resides with his wife and children, two daughters and a son. This son, Harry, although but twenty, is a famous rider, and Captain Jack is specially proud of his abilities as a "roper," he having on one occasion thrown a wild steer and tied him in forty-seven and a half seconds from the word "go," a record which has never been equalled by the most expert cow boy in the West.

As has been before stated, Captain Crawford has never tasted liquor, and his reason for it, as given by himself, shows both the affectionate and resolute side of his character. He says:

"Through my father's one great failing, intemperance, I was deprived of most everything that a boy should have had. When my mother lay on her death-bed she called me to her, and placing her hand on my head, she whispered: 'Johnny, my son, my wild and reckless boy, you know how much your mother loves you. I am going to heaven, my boy, and I want you to give me a promise that I may take it hence with me. Promise that you will never drink intoxicating liquors, and it will not be so hard for me to leave this world.' I gave that promise, and amid all the temptations of army and frontier life, whenever I was asked to take a drink, that scene at my Christian mother's bedside came to me, and I was safe."

Captain Crawford is a ready, eloquent and witty speaker, and is in constant request at camp-fires, reunions and temperance meetings, when his duties permit his absence from home.

To the Grand Army of the Republic.

I feel that I can not close these memoirs without referring to the grandest body of men ever banded together for mutual protection, brotherly assistance and mutual comradeship.

Being an invalid, physically helpless, these noble attributes of the Order whose name appears above have been forcibly brought home to me during the years I have been confined to room and bed, and through many a sleepless night have my thoughts reverted to the old heroic days that gave reason for the present existence of the Grand Army of the Republic.

It was born in the storm of battle, nurtured in the weary marches through pestilential swamps under a burning Southern sun, and cemented in the prison stockade, on the deadly skirmish line, at the lonely picket post—for those who were comrades at the front are comrades still, and will be until the last man is mustered out.

These are the "boys" who marched away in the sixties, singing gayly:

> "We are coming, Father Abraham,
> Six hundred thousand more,"

leaving father and mother, wife and children, sweetheart and friends, at their country's call, and whether their brave young lives went out amid the thundering of the guns, or wasted away by fell disease, or they survived to join hands and hearts in after years in the G. A. R., they are the Nation's immortal heroes.

When the mighty armies, whose tramp had been heard around the world, had quietly dissolved, their survivors would come together to talk over the perils they had shared together, and these reunions gradually crystalized into one vast aggregation, banded together in Friendship, Charity and Loyalty.

These are the men whom Lincoln trusted—the men who solved the problem that could only be solved by the sword.

Is it strange that during the tedious hours of the past two years the bright faces of visiting comrades were like rays of sunshine? for I, like the others who wore the blue, am now proud to wear the bronze button of the G. A. R.

The benefits of the Order are most forcibly experienced when sickness or want invades the home, and 'tis then the soldier feels that he is not alone in the world, but is the object of the care and solicitude of his comrades.

When deserted by hope, racked with pain, mental and physical, believing that I would never leave my bed alive, many weary hours of the night have I passed with the "Phantom Army" long since gone to its eternal camping ground; the Army that crossed the River of Life many years ago and is now awaiting the rear guard. In my fancy I found two armies about me, the material and the spiritual, the former composed of comrades whose friendly visits cheered me during the day, the latter my companions of the night. So it was that day or night present or absent comrades contributed to my comfort.

To the living soldier friends my best thanks are due for calls that seemed to relieve me of half the suffering I endured, their very presence a better medicine for body and mind than all the drugs in the pharmacopœia.

And when the last tattoo is sounded and our spirits are called to join the Grand Army gone before, we know that our comrades' loving hands will bear us tenderly to the tomb, and that each recurring year will see our graves blooming with the roses of remembrance while a member of the Grand Army of the Republic survives.

JAMES E. SMITH,
Kit Carson Post, No. 2, Dep't of the Potomac.

THE END.

www.ingramcontent.com/pod-product-compliance
Lightning Source LLC
Chambersburg PA
CBHW032108220426
43664CB00008B/1170